Simple Faith

BIBLE STUDY GUIDE

From the Bible-teaching ministry of

Charles R. Swindoll

INSIGHT FOR LIVING

Charles R. Swindoll is a graduate of Dallas Theological Seminary and has served as senior pastor of the First Evangelical Free Church of Fullerton, California, since 1971. Chuck's radio program, "Insight for Living," began in 1979. In addition to his church and radio ministries, Chuck enjoys writing. He has authored numerous books and booklets on a variety of subjects.

Based on the outlines and transcripts of Chuck's sermons, the study guide text is co-authored by Ken Gire, a graduate of Texas Christian University and Dallas Theological Seminary. He also wrote the Living Insights sections.

Editor in Chief:
Cynthia Swindoll

Coauthor of Text:
Ken Gire

Assistant Editor:
Wendy Peterson

Senior Copy Editor:
Marty Anderson

Copy Editors:
Connie Laser and Brown Suffield

Production Artist:
Cindy Ford

Typographer:
Bob Haskins

Director, Communications Division:
Deedee Synder

Project Manager:
Alene Cooper

Project Coordinator:
Susan Nelson

Assistant Print Production Manager:
John Norton

Printer:
Frye and Smith

Unless otherwise identified, all Scripture references are from the New American Standard Bible, © The Lockman Foundation 1960, 1962, 1963, 1968, 1971, 1972, 1973, 1975, 1977. Used by permission. Other translations cited are The Revised English Bible [REB], The Living Bible [TLB] and King James Version [KJV].

An effort has been made to locate sources and obtain permission where necessary for the quotations used in this book. In the event of any unintentional omission, a modification will gladly be incorporated in future printings.

ISBN 0-8499-8406-8

Printed in the United States of America.

COVER ILLUSTRATION: Robert Gantt Steele.

CONTENTS

1   Let's Keep it Simple   1
     Survey of Matthew 5–7

2   The Qualities of Simple Faith   8
     Matthew 5:1–12

3   A Simple Counterstrategy: Shake and Shine   19
     Matthew 5:13–16

4   Simplicity Starts from Within   28
     Matthew 5:17–26; 15:1–20

5   Simple Instructions on Serious Issues   36
     Matthew 5:27–37; 19:3, 7–8

6   Simple Advice to the Selfish and Strong-willed   44
     Matthew 5:38–48

7   Beware! Religious Performance Now Showing   54
     Matthew 6:1–8; Micah 6:6–8

8   Prayer and Fasting Minus All the Pizzazz   64
     Matthew 6:9–18

9   When Simple Faith Erodes   72
     Matthew 6:19–24

10   The Subtle Enemy of Simple Faith   81
     Matthew 6:25–34; Luke 10:38–42

11   If You're Serious about Simple Faith, Stop This!   89
     Matthew 7:1–5; Galatians 6:1

12   The Most Powerful of All Four-letter Words   98
     Matthew 7:6–12

13   Simple Yet Serious Warnings for Complicated Times .   108
     Matthew 7:13–23

14   The Simple Secret of an Unsinkable Life   116
     Matthew 7:24–29

Books for Probing Further   123

Ordering Information/Order Form   127

INTRODUCTION

For too many Christians, life has become an exhausting, demanding series of relentless responsibilities . . . a marathon of misery. Trying to fulfill the expectations of fellow believers, well-meaning friends, and hard-charging religious leaders, more and more people are losing the joy of walking with Christ in simple faith.

Unfortunately, the tyranny of the urgent mixed with these legalistic demands of modern-day Pharisees have stolen the delights from many a heart, leaving the ranks of Christianity marked by a collection of grim, guilty, and defeated saints. Surprising though it may seem, that is the same situation Jesus encountered in the first century when He began to minister to those who had been impacted by the scribes and the Pharisees. How few understood what it meant to live in grace!

Our Lord's Sermon on the Mount was, therefore, His strong statement against graceless living. His words were not only revolutionary then, they remain so today. By stripping away all the hypocrisy and complicated requirements of man-made religions, He provides fresh hope and true freedom.

As we return to this masterpiece of biblical truth, may Christ's teaching introduce you to new dimensions of a life worth living, a life of simple faith.

Chuck Swindoll

Chuck Swindoll

PUTTING TRUTH INTO ACTION

Knowledge apart from application falls short of God's desire for His children. He wants us to apply what we learn so that we will change and grow. This study guide was prepared with these goals in mind. As you go through the following pages, we hope your desire to discover biblical truth will grow as your understanding of God's Word increases, and that you will be encouraged to apply what you've learned.

To assist you in your study, we've included a section called **Living Insights** at the end of each lesson. These exercises will challenge you to study further and to think of specific ways to put your discoveries into action.

There are many ways to use this guide—in personal devotions, group studies, discussions with friends and family, and Sunday school classes. And, of course, it's an ideal study aid when you're listening to its corresponding "Insight for Living" radio series.

To benefit most from this study guide, we would encourage you to consider it a spiritual journal. That's why we've included space in the **Living Insights** for recording your thoughts and discoveries. We hope you'll return to those sections often for review and encouragement as you continue to grow in your walk with Christ.

Ken Gire

Ken Gire
Coauthor of Text
Author of Living Insights

Simple Faith

Chapter 1

LET'S KEEP IT SIMPLE

Survey of Matthew 5–7

Like the Phantom of the Opera, hypocrisy hides its disfigured face under a mask, striving to conceal its true ugliness. Yet despite its hideousness, hypocrisy is addictive—the more we wear the mask, the more accustomed we become to its appearance.

The term *hypocrite* is taken from the ancient Greek stage. Often, an actor would have to perform several parts through the course of a play, the different roles signaled by various masks. He might place a humorous mask in front of him and rattle off a few sidesplitting lines of comedy. Then he would go to the side of the stage and get another mask, perhaps one of sorrow or sadness, and pour out some heart-wrenching lines of tragedy.

The actor was called a *hupocritēs*, which is transliterated into the English word *hypocrite*. As time passed, the etymology of the word evolved to become a synonym for three things. First, it was used to describe someone who participated in an artificial role, one who lived an unreal life behind a mask. Second, it came to be used to describe someone who concealed true motives under a cloak of pretense. Third, it came to mean an individual who hid a hideous heart beneath a righteous exterior.

No sin is more strongly denounced in all the Scriptures than hypocrisy—Jesus Himself reserved His most scathing rebukes for it—yet none is more universally practiced.

Our Times: Display of Gross Hypocrisy

In our day, we have seen hypocrisy in the political, moral, financial, ethical and, yes, even the religious realms. It flourishes in an environment where packaging is more important than product, where image is more essential than truth, where style is more significant than substance.

1

Though most of us practice hypocrisy in some form or another, when it is exposed in others, we become enraged. We may be grateful for services rendered that appear thorough, but when we strip away the veneer and find we've been ripped off by some contractor who has cut corners, we become suspicious of all service people. The same thing can happen in the religious realm. In the name of God, sermons can be preached, prayers offered, funds raised, buildings created. But if we find that the preacher is a hypocrite, we are outraged and can eventually become jaded toward religion.

Jesus' Sermon on the Mount, beautifully bold in its authenticity, strips off the hypocritical masks of those who strut their self-righteous stuff for everyone to see and applaud. More lofty and also more stringent than the code given to Moses on the peaks of Mount Sinai, the Sermon on the Mount is not so much a code of human behavior as it is a character sketch of the Christlike life. But before we begin our ascent up this mount, let's briefly survey our terrain.

Jesus' Words: A Plea for True Righteousness

The Sermon on the Mount can be read in only fifteen minutes, yet it encapsulates authentic righteousness better than any other that's ever been preached. Behind Jesus' uncompromising words is a heartfelt concern for those who had been taught to substitute the artificial for the authentic. They had been led astray by an ensemble cast of hypocrites—Israel's religious leaders. Regarding these leaders, Jesus articulates the key to His sermon: "Do not be like them" (Matt. 6:8). The great admonition that resounds through both testaments is that God's people are to be different from the world around them.

> "You shall not do what is done in the land of Egypt
> where you lived, nor are you to do what is done in
> the land of Canaan where I am bringing you; you
> shall not walk in their statutes." (Lev. 18:3)

But God's people have often treated that admonition with casual and cavalier disregard.

> They did not destroy the peoples,
> As the Lord commanded them,
> But they mingled with the nations,
> And learned their practices,
> And served their idols,

2

Which became a snare to them.
(Ps. 106:34–36)

Jesus' sermon to His followers was merely an echo of His Father's commands to Israel.[1] They were to be different from the world around them. Different in how they solved their conflicts. Different in how they ran their businesses. Different in how they responded to affliction. What is so appealing about hypocrisy is that it provides us with an opportunity to travel down both sides of the street. We can appear to be walking the straight and narrow path of righteousness on the outside, but on the inside we're skipping down a wide thoroughfare of wickedness. The Pharisees were masters at this. Most people saw only their righteous facade, not the wickedness they sheltered in their hearts. That's why the command in Matthew 5:20 undoubtedly evoked a collective gasp from the crowd.

> "For I say to you, that unless your righteousness surpasses that of the scribes and Pharisees, you shall not enter the kingdom of heaven."

The crowd of people scratched their heads. How could *their* righteousness exceed that of the scribes and Pharisees? After all, wasn't obedience to the Law the consuming passion of these religious leaders? Hadn't they proved their devotion to righteousness by taking the original Ten Commandments and breaking them down to 250 commandments and 365 prohibitions? How could anyone's righteousness exceed that?

Jesus answers this last question with four directives of simple faith found in Matthew 5–7. As we zero in on each chapter, the purposes of this unparalleled preacher are placed in perspective.

Out with Hypocrisy!

Chapter 5 falls neatly into three parts, each answering a question: What does it mean to have character? (vv. 3–12); What does it mean to make an impact? (vv. 13–16); What does it mean to be godly? (vv. 17–48).[2]

---

1. For further evidence of God's admonition and His people's disregard, see 1 Samuel 8:5, 19–20; Ezekiel 5:7–8; 20:7–8, 32; Jeremiah 10:2; 2 Kings 17:7–8.

2. Six different times in these verses there are contrasts between what has been previously said and what Jesus says (Matt. 5:21–22, 27–28, 31–32, 33–34, 38–39, 43–44).

Down with Performance!

Chapter 6 reaches over and jerks the masks off pride and anxiety. Jesus warns that pride can infiltrate even the holiest of acts: giving (vv. 2–4), praying (vv. 5–15), and fasting (vv. 16–18). He warns that our righteous deeds should not be performed for an earthly audience but for an audience of one in heaven (vv. 1, 4, 6, 18). In the remainder of the chapter, Jesus unmasks a preoccupation with material security as a lack of trust in the Father to provide (vv. 19–34).

Up with Tolerance!

Chapter 7:1–5 soundly condemns a judgmental attitude and echoes forth tolerance. A tolerance capable of embracing others with differing backgrounds, lifestyles, or styles of worship.

On with Commitment!

The final illustrations—commitment to the Gospel in verse 6, to prayer in verses 7–11, and to the truth in the remainder of the chapter—impress upon us that it isn't enough to merely say "Lord, Lord . . ." Hypocrites do that. Nor is it enough to merely listen to His Word. Hypocrites do that too. For our righteousness to exceed that of the scribes and Pharisees, we must mean what we say (vv. 21–23) and do what we hear (vv. 24–27).

End of sermon. Short, simple, and to the point. Not so much as a wasted word. And how did the crowd respond to His penetrating words?

> The result was that when Jesus had finished these words, the multitudes were *amazed* at His teaching; for He was teaching them as one having authority, and not as their scribes. (7:28–29, emphasis added)

My Response: An Admission before Almighty God

Jesus concluded His call to simple faith with an altar call, so to speak. He did not want the crowd to merely listen to His words, but to live them. And He wants no less from us. But we must admit a few things to God before we can begin to make any changes in our lives. Let's each start by being unrelentingly open, honest, and to the point, and then confessing:

I am not completely free of hypocrisy. I often play a part, act out a role, wear a mask. I wear the mask of a clown to hide the tragedies in my life. I wear the mask of a hero to hide the villain who lurks within.

I do not always search my motives. When I do, I find that they are often misguided, manipulative, and occasionally even malicious.

I have not stopped judging others. I am tolerant of the logs in my own eyes and yet so intolerant of the specks in the eyes of other people. My condescending gaze often stems from a heart full of pride.

I dare not continue as I am. As I sit here shocked and convicted, I realize I need help.

The Sermon on the Mount wasn't meant to warm our hearts with flowery rhetoric. It was meant to radically change our lives by first bringing us to our knees. Jesus didn't accomplish that with a long-winded sermon. He did it with a few well-chosen paragraphs. Short. Simple. But sincere. Just like the few, finely honed paragraphs spoken centuries later at a dedication ceremony.

On November 19, 1863, two men came to Pennsylvania to dedicate a Union cemetery: the patriotic orator, Edward Everett, and the President of the United States, Abraham Lincoln. Everett went first and waxed eloquent for one hour and fifty-seven minutes. Lincoln ascended the podium next and spoke for a total of two minutes. History does not remember Everett's speech, but it will never forget Lincoln's Gettysburg Address.

The same could be said of the Sermon on the Mount. Certainly longer and more eloquent sermons have been given. The entire message, from introduction to altar call, takes only fifteen minutes to read. Yet the world will never forget its poetic beauty, poignant images, and powerful conclusion.

 ## Living Insights STUDY ONE

Take some time now to read the sermon at one sitting. Try to imagine yourself in the crowd, hearing these words for the very first time.

Are you confused by any verses? Which ones?

_____

_____

Explain why.

_____

_____

Are you convicted by any verses? Which ones?

Explain why.

Are you comforted by any verses? Which ones?

Explain why.

 Living Insights

Now that you've read over the entire sermon, try your hand at charting its structure. Begin by summarizing the contents of each chapter, then jot down any key words or phrases you find insightful.

The Sermon on the Mount
Matthew 5–7

	CHAPTER 5	CHAPTER 6	CHAPTER 7
Major topics and their verses			
Key words or phrases			

Chapter 2

THE QUALITIES OF SIMPLE FAITH

Matthew 5:1–12

Try to think of some great preachers and a flood of names fills your mind: Dwight L. Moody, H. A. Ironside, Donald Grey Barnhouse, Charles Haddon Spurgeon, John Wesley, Peter Marshall. Now try thinking of some great sermons. The flood of thoughts trickles to a stop, doesn't it? Most likely, only one comes to mind— the Sermon on the Mount.

Of all the sermons ever preached, this one stands as the pinnacle of sermonic perfection. Like the "Moonlight Sonata," there is not one extraneous note. It occupies only three chapters in the Bible, yet it has inspired countless volumes of exegesis and exposition, not to mention reams of changed lives.

Each facet of the sermon sparkles like an exquisitely cut jewel, flashes of truth glinting from it with almost blinding brilliance. Today we want to squint with a jeweler's eye at one facet of that sermon—the Beatitudes. For it is here that we will behold the flawless qualities of simple faith.

Initial Observations of Jesus' Words

Matthew describes the setting of this jewel in 5:1–2.

> And when He saw the multitudes, He went up on the mountain; and after He sat down, His disciples came to Him. And opening His mouth He began to teach them.

Before we scrutinize the main body of Jesus' sermon, let's make a few initial observations from Matthew's introduction. First, *Jesus delivered the sermon outside rather than inside,* without notes or voice amplification, which is probably why He went up on a hill. Second, *He sat down rather than stood up,* so that His presence, while powerful, would not be overpowering. He would remain approachable, touchable, believable. Third, *He taught rather than preached.* Sermons that stick have substance, not simply a dynamic delivery. The Sermon on the Mount is a textbook example of substantive teaching, systematized and logically arranged. Fourth, as we scan the Beatitudes, we find that *Jesus blessed the crowd rather than rebuking them.* Nine times He repeated the introductory benediction, perhaps in an effort to underscore to His hearers the divine blessings available to them.

Fresh Fruit from the Beatitudes

As we examine verses 3–12, we want to raise a couple of general questions about these blessings and then get into a specific analysis of each individual character quality Jesus stressed.

General Questions

First, *What is meant by the term "blessed"?* The Greek term is *makarios,* which, in the extrabiblical literature of that day, was used to describe two different things. One was the social stratum of the wealthy, who, by virtue of their riches, lived above the workaday worries of the rest of the world. The other was the condition of the Greek gods, who were contented because they had everything they desired. In the Sermon on the Mount, Jesus says that His own followers will be just as happy as the pantheon of pagan gods and the privileged aristocracy. Their contentment and fulfillment, however, is not derived from power and wealth but from possessing an inner confidence that comes from traveling down the right road (see Ps. 1:1–2).

The second question we need to ask about the Beatitudes is, *Are the blessings for now or later?* Since the first beatitude (v. 3) and the eighth (v. 10) offer blessings in the present tense, while the other six offer blessings in the future tense, the best answer would be, "Both now and later." They form the guidelines of authentic Christian character that have a present as well as a future fulfillment.

Brief Analysis of the Beatitudes

The first beatitude is found in verse 3:

> "Blessed are the poor in spirit, for theirs is the kingdom of heaven."

The poverty referred to here has nothing to do with material destitution or financial insecurity. Rather, it describes a contrite and humble spirit that acknowledges its spiritual bankruptcy before God.[1]

1. Compare Luke 18:9–14 and Revelation 3:14–17.

That great hymn "Rock of Ages" poetically describes this spirit:

> Nothing in my hand I bring,
> Simply to Thy cross I cling;
> Naked, come to Thee for dress,
> Helpless, look to Thee for grace;
> Foul, I to the fountain fly,
> Wash me, Savior, or I die![2]

The blessing reserved for these humble people is nothing less than "the kingdom of heaven." They will enter into a new way of life where the King will guide, guard, and direct them.

In verse 4 we discover the second beatitude:

> "Blessed are those who mourn, for they shall be comforted."

The word used here is the strongest Greek term for *mourn*, meaning "a passionate lament." It describes the sorrow of a broken heart, the ache of a longing soul, the anguish of a troubled mind. Its tears may fall over broad territory, ranging from the evil in the world to the personal loss of a loved one. Contextually, it most likely refers to a passionate spirit of contrition, much like Paul's in Romans 7:24: "Wretched man that I am! Who will set me free from the body of this death?"[3]

The blessing extended to the brokenhearted is the salve of God's comfort. God promises to be near them (Ps. 34:18) and to bind up the wound of their broken hearts (Isa. 61:1).

The third beatitude is found in verse 5:

> "Blessed are the gentle, for they shall inherit the earth."

All too often the immediate images that come to mind when we hear the word *gentle* are "wimp" and "doormat." But in Jesus' day, this word had a much different connotation. It was used to describe a wild stallion that had been brought under control, words

---

2. Augustus J. Toplady, "Rock of Ages," in *The Hymnal for Worship and Celebration* (Waco, Tex.: Word Music, 1986), no. 204.

3. It is important to clarify here that merely admitting sin is not tantamount to confession. Neither is confession equivalent to contrition. Contrition is mourning over sin, grieving with brokenness over the hurt that sin has caused. We see this grief both in David's repentance of his sin with Bathsheba (compare Ps. 32:3–5 with 51:17) and in Peter's realization of his denial of Christ (Luke 22:61–62).

that soothed strong emotions, or an ointment that took fever out of a wound. In one of Plato's works, a child asks a physician to be tender with him. The word the child uses is *gentle*. Those who are polite, courteous, and treat others with dignity are termed "gentle." Matthew later uses the word to describe the Lord Jesus (11:29; 21:5). The blessing associated with this trait is the inheritance of the land.[4] Unlike the Roman empire, the kingdom of God was not one that could be possessed by might but by meekness.

The fourth beatitude is found in verse 6:

> "Blessed are those who hunger and thirst for righteousness, for they shall be satisfied."

This beatitude describes those with an unquenchable thirst to know more about God and His Word, those who long to drink deeply from the fountain of truth (Ps. 42:2; 63:1). It describes those with an insatiable hunger for fellowship with God (Amos 8:11–14).

The promise to those with this burning thirst and gnawing hunger is just what you would expect from a loving father—"they shall be *satisfied*" (Matt. 7:7–11; Ps. 107:9). A. T. Robertson says this word is derived from the word for fodder or grain and, therefore, came to mean "to feed or fatten cattle."[5] Like hefty, well-fed livestock, these people will be satisfied.

As we turn to look at the fifth blessing, we'll notice a subtle shift in focus. Just as the first tablet of the Ten Commandments concentrated on our relationship with God and the second on our relationship with people, so it is with the Sermon on the Mount. John Stott notes:

> In the second half of the beatitudes (the last four) we seem to turn even more from our attitude to God to our attitude to our fellow human beings.[6]

---

4. "The verb 'inherit' often relates to entrance into the Promised Land (e.g., Deut. 4:1; 16:20; cf. Isa. 57:13; 60:21). . . . Entrance into the Promised Land ultimately became a pointer toward entrance into the new heaven *and the new earth* . . . the consummation of the messianic kingdom." D. A. Carson, "Matthew," *The Expositor's Bible Commentary* (Grand Rapids, Mich.: Zondervan Publishing House, 1984), vol. 8, pp. 133–34.

5. A. T. Robertson, *Word Pictures in the New Testament* (Nashville, Tenn.: Broadman Press, 1930), vol. 1, p. 41.

6. John R. W. Stott, *The Message of the Sermon on the Mount (Matthew 5–7)*, rev. ed. of *Christian Counter-Culture*, The Bible Speaks Today series (1978; Downers Grove, Ill.: Inter-Varsity Press, n.d.), p. 47.

With that in mind, let's look at the fifth beatitude now, which is found in verse 7:

> "Blessed are the merciful, for they shall receive mercy."

Mercy is a concern for people in need that goes beyond sympathy to empathy. A merciful person sees what the suffering see and feels what they feel (see Heb. 13:3). True mercy never stops with an outpouring of emotion; it stoops to offer help (compare James 2:15–16; 1 John 3:17). It is a Good Samaritan attitude that assists those who suffer the consequences of sin, pain, misery, or distress (Luke 10:30–37).

The promise to these people is bushels of mercy, harvested from the seeds of mercy they have sown to others. Those who remain detached and unmoved when others are in need will receive like treatment (Prov. 21:13). But those who extend themselves, entering into the world of another's pain, will receive the same compassion from the Lord and others (Prov. 19:17).

The sixth beatitude is found in verse 8:

> "Blessed are the pure in heart, for they shall see God."

Perhaps "utterly sincere" would be the best description of this type of person. It pictures someone whose entire life is free from hypocrisy and is lived transparently before God and others, someone who has no guile or hidden motives.[7] The blessing reserved for the utterly sincere is a resplendent one: "they shall see God." John Stott also comments on this glorious promise:

> Only the pure in heart will see God, see him now with the eye of faith and see his glory in the hereafter, for only the utterly sincere can bear the dazzling vision in whose light the darkness of deceit must vanish and by whose fire all shams are burned up.[8]

The seventh beatitude is found in verse 9:

> "Blessed are the peacemakers, for they shall be called sons of God."

---

7. How this must have stuck in the craw of the Pharisees, whose duplicitous lives were covered over with the dross of deception (Matt. 23:25–28).

8. Stott, *Sermon on the Mount*, p. 49.

Peacemakers never seek conflict. They release tension, rather than increase it. They seek solutions, not arguments. They generate light, not heat. They are "quick to hear, slow to speak, and slow to anger" (James 1:19), quick with the gentle word that averts wrath (Prov. 15:1).

Make no mistake, however; peacemaker is not a synonym for appeaser. To overlook flagrant sin or embrace doctrinal heresy for the sake of peace only cheapens it. This is not peace at any price. Luke 17:3 says, "If your brother sins, rebuke him; and if he repents, forgive him." It cheapens peace to treat a gross offense lightly when there's no contrite heart of repentance.

What is the royal blessing conferred on true peacemakers? They will be called the sons of God, for when they reconcile those alienated from each other, they most reflect the character of their heavenly Father (2 Cor. 5:18–19).

The final beatitude is found in verses 10–12:

> "Blessed are those who have been persecuted for the sake of righteousness, for theirs is the kingdom of heaven. Blessed are you when men cast insults at you, and persecute you, and say all kinds of evil against you falsely, on account of Me. Rejoice, and be glad, for your reward in heaven is great, for so they persecuted the prophets who were before you."

The persecution that's in view here comes as a result of our faith—not because we've simply been offensive or fanatical or opinionated. Persecution results when two irreconcilable value systems collide. When that happens, people will revile you, pursue you, and lie about you in an attempt to extinguish the light that reveals the dark, cobwebbed corners of their lives.

The best response in such situations is not to recoil or retaliate in the face of rejection but to rejoice. Why? Because, ultimately, a heavenly reward awaits you. And because, historically, you belong to a noble succession of prophets who suffered in the same manner. Everyone likes to be accepted and respected, but universal popularity is as much a hallmark of false prophets as persecution is of true ones (Luke 6:26).

Never forget that the world, whose favor we sometimes court, is at odds with God (James 4:4). He exalts the humble, not the proud. He ascribes greatness to servants, not to masters. He is not impressed with pomp and ceremony, but with things done quietly, motivated by a pure heart. The world honors the beautiful and the brilliant, the skilled and the strong, the great and the gifted. But God reaches out and blesses the weak and the withered, publicans and prostitutes, tax-collectors and thieves.

A Couple of Suggestions for Applying Jesus' Words

The Beatitudes come to us like a big box of interrelated character qualities labeled "Assembly Required." The task of assembling the component parts of Christlike character can be overwhelming. But instead of becoming intimidated, let's roll up our sleeves and tackle the project a step at a time.

Whip out your weekly planner and work the Beatitudes into your schedule, a day at a time. On Monday, work on dependence, being poor in spirit. On Tuesday, concentrate on repentance. On Wednesday, take on gentleness. On Thursday, focus on the pursuit of truth. On Friday, mercy. Saturday, integrity. Sunday, peacemaking. Then come full circle to the next Monday and try rejoicing. But don't think you'll build Christlike character into your life with a week's worth of self-improvement projects. Keep that eight-day cycle rolling along for the rest of your life, because that's what it will take.

Here's another idea for putting this message on the Beatitudes to practical use. Start noticing the contrast between the Sermon on the Mount and the subliminal sermon the world preaches. Sit in front of your television like a Doberman pinscher and intently observe the lifestyles of the rich and famous. What do you see? You see people merging their way to corporate empires, padding their pockets en route. You see black hearts sheathed in white evening gowns, sleeping their way to their ambitions. You see Oscars clutched like idols by screen gods preening in the limelight. In short, you see a world turned upside down—a world that has its own set of beatitudes:

> Happy are the "pushers": for they get on in the world.
> Happy are the hard-boiled: for they never let life hurt them.
> Happy are they who complain: for they get their own way in the end.
> Happy are the blasé: for they never worry over their sins.
> Happy are the slave-drivers: for they get results.
> Happy are the knowledgeable men of the world: for they know their way around.

Happy are the trouble-makers: for they make people
take notice of them.[9]

God offers a better world, but He will have to turn us right-side
up before we will be able to see it. And He turns us right-side up
with the Beatitudes.

🍇 *Living Insights*

Before we can assemble a Christlike character, we need a clear
idea of where to begin. So let's take some time now to honestly
evaluate how much the Beatitudes are a part of our lives.

On a one-to-ten scale, ten being the character of Christ,

• How poor in spirit are you?

$$1 \quad 2 \quad 3 \quad 4 \quad 5 \quad 6 \quad 7 \quad 8 \quad 9 \quad 10$$

What could you do to move that a notch higher?

_____

_____

• How deeply do you mourn over sin?

$$1 \quad 2 \quad 3 \quad 4 \quad 5 \quad 6 \quad 7 \quad 8 \quad 9 \quad 10$$

Why do you think that number isn't any higher?

_____

_____

• How gentle are you?

$$1 \quad 2 \quad 3 \quad 4 \quad 5 \quad 6 \quad 7 \quad 8 \quad 9 \quad 10$$

What usually causes you to lose your self-control and become
less gentle?

_____

_____

9. J. B. Phillips, *Good News: Thoughts on God and Man* (New York, N.Y.: Macmillan Co.,
1963), pp. 33–34.

- How greatly do you hunger and thirst for righteousness?

    1 2 3 4 5 6 7 8 9 10

  How do you think your spiritual appetite can be increased?

  _____

  _____

- How merciful are you?

    1 2 3 4 5 6 7 8 9 10

  What kinds of situations bring out this quality in you and what kinds stifle it?

  _____

  _____

- How pure is your heart?

    1 2 3 4 5 6 7 8 9 10

  Describe any discrepancies between your public self and your private self.

  _____

  _____

- How much of a peacemaker are you?

    1 2 3 4 5 6 7 8 9 10

  What are a few things you could do to cultivate this quality?

  _____

  _____

- How joyful are you in the midst of persecution?

    1 2 3 4 5 6 7 8 9 10

  When you experience persecution, what usually prompts it?

  _____

  _____

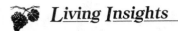

Deep-dish, home-baked apple pie. As the tantalizing aroma wisps its way through the house, your mouth starts to water. The whiff leads to a bite, and before long you're scraping the plate with your fork, scavenging for any loose crumbs and begging for the recipe.

True Christlike character is like that apple pie. When we see the recipe of the Beatitudes fleshed out in the life of someone around us, it whets our appetite.

Thumb through the following recipe file of the eight qualities listed in Matthew 5:3–12. Next to each one, write in the name of somebody you know who best incarnates that quality in his or her life. Then write out what that person says or does to create the tantalizing whiff of Christlikeness. You may not be able to link every quality to a person, but complete as many as you can.

_____ is poor in spirit.

How? _____

_____

_____ mourns.

How? _____

_____

_____ is gentle.

How? _____

_____

_____ hungers and thirsts for righteousness.

How? _____

_____

_____ is merciful.

How? _____

_____

_____ is pure in heart.

How? _____

_____

_____ is a peacemaker.

How? _____

_____

_____ rejoices in the midst of persecution.

How? _____

_____

Of this group of people, who has most enticed you to want to know more about the recipe of Christlikeness?

_____

Why don't you take a few minutes now to write or call this person and express your feelings of gratitude for the effect he or she has had on your life.

Chapter 3

A SIMPLE COUNTERSTRATEGY: SHAKE AND SHINE

Matthew 5:13–16

More than two hundred fifty years ago Isaac Watts posed some searching questions in a hymn he wrote. In every generation that followed, those questions went begging for answers. They go begging still today.

> Am I a soldier of the cross,
> A follower of the Lamb?
> And shall I fear to own His cause
> Or blush to speak His name?
>
> Must I be carried to the skies
> On flowery beds of ease,
> While others fought to win the prize
> And sailed through bloody seas?
>
> Are there no foes for me to face?
> Must I not stem the flood?
> Is this vile world a friend to grace,
> To help me on to God?[1]

Dwell on that last question, will you? Is this vile world a friend of grace? Will it help you on to God if you listen to its counsel? If you sit at the feet of its professors, if you read its books, if you watch its films, if you learn its ways, if you march to the beat of its drum, will it help you on to God?

The setting of Isaac Watts' hymn is a battlefield. If you read the lyrics, you can almost hear the angry report of cannon in the distance and smell the acrid lingering of gunpowder in the air. You can almost see the blood trickling crimson from a soldier's wound. But that kind of warfare is only a pale metaphor of a greater battle— a battle in which invisible warriors draw their sabers over the human soul. That warfare is spiritual, fought not against flesh and blood but against the entrenched powers of the demonic hierarchy (Eph. 6:12).

1. Isaac Watts, "Am I a Soldier of the Cross?" in *Hymns for the Family of God* (Nashville, Tenn.: Paragon Associates, 1976), no. 411.

These spiritual adversaries are also as strategic as they are strong. They know where our Achilles' heel is, and they aim their arrows accordingly. The volley can come anytime and from anywhere. And it can fly from any number of worldly bows.

"No," Isaac Watts would have us answer, "this vile world will not help me on to God; it will only hinder me."

The Plain Truth about the Real World

Because the world system is degenerate and antithetical to the things of God (1 John 5:19), we should not love the world (2:15–17). It is our enemy, bent on barring the path in our walk with God.

What can we expect from such a world? Persecution and tribulation (John 15:20, 16:33). Why? Generally, because this world rests in the lap of the Evil One. Specifically, because it hates Christ. Watts' question leads to a deeper one. Since this vile world is no friend of grace, what kind of people should we be as we live in this hostile environment?

Jesus answers that question for us in the Beatitudes (Matt. 5:3–12). The strongest weapon against such formidable opposition is an equally strong character.

But how can soldiers of the cross—armed only with humility, contrition, gentleness, a longing for righteousness, mercy, purity, and peace—ever make a lasting impact on a world that's tough, hostile and, as Watts described it, even vile? The same way Jesus did. He was armed with those same characteristics, opposed by an even more hostile world. His only response to its hatred was love; to its lies was truth; to its harshness, gentleness; to its cross, forgiveness. With these qualities, He triumphed over His opposition.

So the only way for us to make a lasting impact on the world is to do what Jesus did—be distinct, not identical. Therein lies the genius of our counterstrategy. As Dr. Martyn Lloyd-Jones noted:

> The glory of the gospel is that when the Church is absolutely different from the world, she invariably attracts it. It is then that the world is made to listen to her message, though it may hate it at first.[2]

That explains how Jesus could look into the faces of a handful of Palestinian peasants and call them the salt of the earth, the light

---

2. D. Martyn Lloyd-Jones, *Studies in the Sermon on the Mount* (1959; reprint [2 vols. in 1], Grand Rapids, Mich.: William B. Eerdmans Publishing Co., 1971), p. 37.

of the world (vv. 13–16). For they would impact the world in a dramatic way. Not by their greatness but by their gentleness. Not by their might but by their meekness. Not by their charisma but by their contrition.

The Only Strategy That Works in the World

In Matthew 5:13–16, Jesus uses two domestic metaphors to show how Christians impact the world. But before we can understand these images, we must first understand two things about the world into which they were set.

Two Facts about the World

This world is in a process of decay. Isaac Watts called it vile. The apostle Paul takes it a step further.

> Do all things without grumbling or disputing; that you may prove yourselves to be blameless and inno-cent, children of God above reproach in the midst of a crooked and perverse generation, among whom you appear as lights in the world. (Phil. 2:14–16)

Crooks and perverts. Hyperbole? Sensationalistic, tabloid journalism? Not if we take Romans 3 seriously.

> "There is none righteous, not even one;
> There is none who understands,
> There is none who seeks for God;
> All have turned aside, together they have become
>   useless;
> There is none who does good,
> There is not even one."
> "Their throat is an open grave,
> With their tongues they keep deceiving,"
> "The poison of asps is under their lips";
> "Whose mouth is full of cursing and bitterness";
> "Their feet are swift to shed blood,
> Destruction and misery are in their paths,
> And the path of peace have they not known."
> "There is no fear of God before their eyes."
> (vv. 10–18)

The world is also enveloped in spiritual darkness. The depths of this darkness can scarcely be exaggerated. Those who sit in this darkness not only are blind to the truth but recoil from any light the truth shines in their eyes. In this moral blackness the emotions range from boredom to despair, from a tasteless existence to a hopeless one. Within that prison sin's consequences scurry around like disgusting insects. These infest every nook and cranny of that prison, lying in wait in its dank labyrinths.

Looking deeply into the eyes of His followers, Jesus refused to address those problems in great detail. Instead, He chose "You are the salt. . . . You are the light," to emphasize the solution. In both Matthew 5:13–14, the "you" is emphatic, alerting us to the importance of our responsibility to be involved. One further observation on those two verses: the verb is in the present tense. Salt and light are not something we *become*; they're something we *are*. If you are a Christian you are both. But to be effective we must do two things— give the world a better taste of the salt and a closer look at the light.

A Better Taste of the Salt

> "You are the salt of the earth; but if the salt has become tasteless, how will it be made salty again? It is good for nothing anymore, except to be thrown out and trampled under foot by men." (v. 13)

In ancient days, salt was the most common preservative known. Fishermen would use it to preserve their catch, spreading it between layers of fish as a seal to ward off decay from bacteria. Even in frontier America our forefathers depended on salted meat in their trek across the continent. Meats soaked in brine or rubbed with salt were "cured" and thus were restrained from rotting.

Besides acting as a preservative, salt also adds flavor and creates thirst. It adds "bite" to our food. However, it can lose that bite— "become tasteless" in Jesus' words. John Stott explains how this can happen.

> Now, strictly speaking, salt can never lose its salt- ness. I am given to understand that sodium chloride is a very stable chemical compound, which is resis- tant to nearly every attack. Nevertheless, it can be- come contaminated by mixture with impurities, and then it becomes useless, even dangerous. Desalted salt is unfit even for manure, *i.e.* the compost heap. Dr. David Turk has suggested to me that what was [in Jesus' day] popularly called "salt" was in fact a

white powder (perhaps from around the Dead Sea) which, while containing sodium chloride, also contained much else, since, in those days, there were no refineries. Of this dust the sodium chloride was probably the most soluble component and so the most easily washed out. The residue of white powder still looked like salt, and was doubtless still called salt, but it neither tasted nor acted like salt. It was just road dust.[3]

As Christ's preserving agents in a decaying world, we must retain our "saltness" . . . and shake that salt around!

A Closer Look at the Light

> "You are the light of the world. A city set on a hill cannot be hidden." (Matt. 5:14)

In a spiritual sense, parts of this world are like the bowels of Carlsbad Caverns, where the darkness is so impenetrable that you can't even see your hand in front of your face. There is not just a loss of vision but a loss of direction. The only remedy for such disorientation is light. Light has one primary function—to dispel darkness. When light appears, your circumstances become illuminated and hope returns as you discover a way out of the cave.

It's comforting to know that there is no darkness so thick that Christ's powerful light cannot penetrate it. The torch that came into the world at the Incarnation, and which has now been handed down from generation to generation of believers, cannot be hidden (John 1:4–5; 8:12; 9:5).

> "Nor do men light a lamp, and put it under the peck-measure, but on the lampstand; and it gives light to all who are in the house." (Matt. 5:15)

This light is indiscriminate in its benefits. Every person "in the house" gets the benefit of the same light. Some in the house like it, some don't, some couldn't care less. But just as it is the nature of light to shine, so it should be with us.

---

3. John R. W. Stott, *The Message of the Sermon on the Mount (Matthew 5–7)*, rev. ed. of *Christian Counter-Culture*, The Bible Speaks Today series (1978; Downers Grove, Ill.: Inter-Varsity Press, n.d.), pp. 59–60.

"Let your light shine before men in such a way that they may see your good works, and glorify your Father who is in heaven." (v. 16)

Jesus doesn't instruct us to sweep the skies with the fanfare of a Hollywood searchlight. He simply wants a quiet shining of our light. And the blacker the darkness, the brighter our light will shine. What is our light? A tent revival where we bring our unsaved friends? No. It is our good works. Not *perfect* works but simply good works. Even *reasonably* good works will do.

> Earl Palmer said once that perhaps the best testimony a Christian couple can give today is a reasonably good marriage. We who are married do not have to pretend we are living as Barbie Dolls on a wedding cake. We have struggles, and dashed expectations too. But if we offer the world a model of a reasonably good marriage, a reasonably good church, a reasonably good college fellowship, it will have radicalizing effects on the world.[4]

What are the good works that bring transformation to the world and glory to God? They are every visible manifestation of our lives, what we say, how we live, the way we treat others, our reactions to trials, the consistency of our faith—everything.

Some Suggestions on Shaking and Shining

In closing, here are three don'ts that will help you become a more positive and effective witness in the world. First, *don't overdo it.* Don't flaunt your light or fling your salt. Don't rub salt into someone's fresh wound and don't shine a flashlight into somebody's eyes. There's no need to be hurtful or offensive. Just shake the salt and keep the light burning in the window.

Second, *don't hold back.* Risk standing alone. See it as your unique opportunity to preserve something that would otherwise decay. Risk getting involved. With prisoners. With addicts. With the homeless. With the handicapped. With unwed mothers. With abused children (see Matt. 25:34–40).

---

4. Rebecca Manley Pippert, *Out of the Saltshaker and into the World* (Downers Grove, Ill.: InterVarsity Press, 1979), p. 162.

Third, *don't worry about the few who resist it.* Remember that the best batters fail two out of every three times they come to bat. Don't let the strikeouts keep you slumped over in the dugout. Nobody bats a thousand. Sometimes the great prophets not only failed to draw a home crowd but were without any fans at all. Some were not only ignored but actively opposed and even martyred . . . "men of whom the world was not worthy" (Heb. 11:35–38). So don't let boos from the bleachers get you down. Keep swinging that bat. Keep shaking that salt and shining that light!

 Living Insights

List some activities you are involved in that give you an opportunity to rub up against the non-Christian world.

1. _____

2. _____

3. _____

4. _____

5. _____

List some non-Christians you pray for regularly.

1. _____

2. _____

3. _____

4. _____

5. _____

Remember, as nice a place as church is, you can spend too much time inside that saltshaker. If your whole life revolves around church activities and Christians, you're living a more sheltered life than is good for you. Or the world.

John Stott asks some searching questions about our involvement in the world.

> God intends us to penetrate the world. Christian salt
> has no business to remain snugly in elegant little

ecclesiastical salt cellars; our place is to be rubbed into the secular community, as salt is rubbed into meat, to stop it going bad. And when society does go bad, we Christians tend to throw up our hands in pious horror and reproach the non-Christian world; but should we not rather reproach ourselves? One can hardly blame unsalted meat for going bad. It cannot do anything else. The real question to ask is: where is the salt?[5]

We can complain about everything from corruption in politics to decadence in movies. But we need to understand that it's a natural process for meat to decay. The real question is: Where is the preserving influence? Where is the salt?

Not all of us can run for Congress or enroll in film school, but we can make a difference where we are—if we get out of the saltshaker.

So for your assignment today, pick up a copy of *Out of the Saltshaker and into the World* by Rebecca Manley Pippert (published by InterVarsity Press). It will give you some practical advice on evangelism as a way of life. It also contains a helpful bibliography of books and booklets that can be given to non-Christians, other books that will help you to organize evangelistic Bible studies, and books on evangelism in general.

Living Insights   STUDY TWO

How are salt and light different from each other?

_____

_____

_____

What do they have in common?

_____

_____

_____

5. Stott, *Sermon on the Mount*, p. 65.

How does our passage for today (Matt. 5:13–16) logically flow out of our previous study (vv. 1–12)?

_____

_____

_____

Read Matthew 25:34–40. List the benevolent activities in those verses.

1. _____

2. _____

3. _____

4. _____

Which of those ministries are you personally (not just financially) involved in?

_____

_____

What activities keep you from being more involved in ministries to the hurting and the helpless?

_____

_____

For each of the four benevolent ministries you listed above, what specific step can you take in the direction of getting more involved?

Ministry	Step of Involvement
1. _____	_____
2. _____	_____
3. _____	_____
4. _____	_____

Chapter 4

SIMPLICITY STARTS FROM WITHIN

Matthew 5:17–26; 15:1–20

Years ago, in a fine book titled *Preaching and Preachers*, Martyn Lloyd-Jones wrote:

> What is preaching? Logic on fire! Eloquent reason! . . . It is theology on fire. And a theology which does not take fire, I maintain, is a defective theology; or at least the man's understanding of it is defective. Preaching is theology coming through a man who is on fire.[1]

We still have the fiery words of great prophets from the past, but because we cannot literally hear their voices or actually watch their gestures, we miss much of the fire that originally burned in and through them. This is especially true of the sermon Jesus delivered on that mountain outside Jerusalem. Talk about a man on fire, the Master was ablaze! Yet it wasn't a fire fueled solely by grandiloquent words. Jesus set the hearts of His hearers on fire that day because He spoke with a burning-bush authority they had never heard or felt before.

"Truly, truly I say unto you . . . ," were His inflammatory words. Words that ignited not only a passion for God but also a consuming controversy concerning Christ's authority and the authority of the Scriptures.

The Authority of the Scriptures

Nothing has ever been spoken with greater authority than God's Holy Word. When a prophet began his message with, "Thus saith the Lord," he was drawing upon the most powerful source of authority known to mankind. Let's look at the nature of this authority, why it was so important, and then examine Christ's relationship to it.

---

1. D. Martyn Lloyd-Jones, *Preaching and Preachers* (Grand Rapids, Mich.: Zondervan Publishing House, 1971), p. 97.

An *authority* is a convincing force. Webster defines it as the "power to influence or command thought, opinion, or behavior."[2] Without it we have no standard. Everyone is left to do what is right in their own eyes (Judg. 21:25).

Prior to Jesus' arrival on the scene, those who spoke for God worked within the framework of the religious establishment and the authority of the Old Testament. But then along came Christ, upsetting the applecart of tradition. He didn't always follow the guidelines prescribed by the Pharisees. For example, he healed on the Sabbath. And He would make authoritative pronouncements prefaced not with the standard, "Thus saith the Lord," but with the more radical "Truly, truly, I say unto you . . ."

The scribes and Pharisees criticized Jesus for doing this because they interpreted His words as setting Himself up as an authority above the sacred Scripture. "He speaks from His own authority," they reasoned among themselves, "and therefore He abolishes the Law."

The Fulfillment of the Law

Jesus silenced His critics by clarifying His relationship to the Law.

The Law and Christ

"Do not think that I came to abolish the Law or the Prophets; I did not come to abolish, but to fulfill." (Matt. 5:17)

Doctrinally, prophetically, and ethically, He did just that: He fulfilled the Law. In His birth, life, death, and resurrection, He brought Scripture to completion. Time and again He would say that His words and actions took place to fulfill what the Lord had spoken by the prophets (see Matt. 12:16–17; 13:13–14, 34–35; 15:7). Then, by obeying every ethical jot and tittle of the Law, Jesus fulfilled the Scripture by living His life in harmony with it.

Jesus emphatically asserted that He was neither above the Law nor in conflict with it. He believed in it fully and kept it faithfully. Furthermore, He didn't pick and choose which parts of the Law were important. To Him, it was all inspired and therefore all important.

"For truly I say to you, until heaven and earth pass away, not the smallest letter or stroke shall pass away from the Law, until all is accomplished." (5:18)

2. *Webster's Ninth New Collegiate Dictionary*, see "authority."

The Law is as enduring as the universe. Both will someday pass away, but until then, the Law will stand unchanged and unthreatened. Jesus emphasized this point by saying that not even "a jot or tittle" will pass away from the Law until all is accomplished.

The word *jot* refers to the smallest letter in the Hebrew alphabet, the yōd, which resembles an apostrophe. The word *tittle* refers to the tiny projection of a Hebrew letter that distinguishes it from a similar letter, much like the upward projection on an *h* distinguishes it from an *n*. So, with those words, "Jesus here upholds the authority of the OT Scriptures right down to the 'least stroke of a pen.'"[3]

Now that we have Christ's relationship to the Law clear in our minds, let's explore the relationship that we, as Christians, should have to it.

The Law and the Christian

> "Whoever then annuls one of the least of these commandments, and so teaches others, shall be called least in the kingdom of heaven; but whoever keeps and teaches them, he shall be called great in the kingdom of heaven." (v. 19)

Verse 19 sets up a contrast between those who casually ignore the Scripture and those who earnestly keep and teach it. There are blessings reserved for the latter group, but consequences for the former. In this verse Jesus reiterates that the authority of the Law remains intact, in spite of the efforts of some to dismantle it. His point is that kingdom living requires the same standard—God's perfect righteousness, as clearly set forth in the Law and the prophets.

Up to now, the crowd was nodding its approval. But verse 20, no doubt, made them flinch.

> "For I say to you, that unless your righteousness surpasses that of the scribes and Pharisees, you shall not enter the kingdom of heaven."

They were probably looking at each other quizzically and whispering, "How could anyone *surpass* the righteousness of the scribes and Pharisees?" Verses 21–26 answer that question. The religious

---

3. D. A. Carson, "Matthew," in *The Expositor's Bible Commentary* (Grand Rapids, Mich.: Zondervan Publishing House, Regency Reference Library, 1984), vol. 8, p. 145.

leaders placed their emphasis on *external appearances;* Christ placed His on *internal character.* They played to the crowd; Jesus, to the audience of the Father. They focused on the rules of the flesh; Christ, on the motivations of the heart. Christ taught that if people were to enter His kingdom, their hearts must first be changed from the inside out, not from the outside in (compare 15:1–20).

So, concerning the Christian's relationship with the Law, it is evident that although we live under a new and better covenant, we should not disregard the moral precepts that lie at the heart of the Old Covenant. Instead, we should strive to deepen our understanding of the spirit that lies behind the letter of the Law. Jesus helps us do that, beginning in verse 21.

The Law and Righteousness

"You have heard that the ancients were told, 'You shall not commit murder' and 'Whoever commits murder shall be liable to the court.'"

The Pharisees taught against the *action* of premeditated murder but not against the *attitude* that spawned it. The way for the people to surpass the righteousness of their religious leaders was not to mow the moral weeds on the surface of their lives but to pull them up by the roots. And the root of murder is anger, as verse 22 indicates.

"But I say to you that everyone who is angry with his brother shall be guilty before the court; and whoever shall say to his brother, 'Raca,' shall be guilty before the supreme court; and whoever shall say 'You fool,' shall be guilty enough to go into the fiery hell."

Although there are cases of justifiable anger,[4] the anger mentioned here is clearly not. It is an anger that sits on a burner of rage and boils over into abuse. It's an "I-wish-he-were-dead" type of anger.

The specific abuse in verse 22 is the word *raca,* an Aramaic term that was equivalent to "empty." We might use the slang word "airhead" in a similar outburst of anger. The next venting of anger is the word "fool," from the Greek term *moros.* As *raca* is a derogatory comment focusing on the person's mental state, *moros* focuses on the moral state.

4. See Ephesians 4:26 and James 1:19.

31

So in this verse we see a progression from anger to abuse. And in the verbal abuse, we see a progression from demeaning a person's intelligence to demeaning the character. The natural course that such comments take is in the direction of murder. If we assassinate character without remorse, could actual murder be very far down the road? By harboring such feelings and pronouncing such judgments, we place *ourselves* on the scales of judgment. With every malicious word we spew forth from our mouths, the balance becomes weighted as an indicting testimony against us.

In verses 23–26, however, Jesus gives us two examples of how to extricate ourselves from the entangling grip of anger.

> "If therefore you are presenting your offering at the altar, and there remember that your brother has something against you, leave your offering there before the altar, and go your way; first be reconciled to your brother, and then come and present your offering. Make friends quickly with your opponent at law while you are with him on the way, in order that your opponent may not deliver you to the judge, and the judge to the officer, and you be thrown into prison. Truly I say to you, you shall not come out of there, until you have paid up the last cent."

The first illustration deals with someone close to us that we have offended.[5] So serious is this breach that Jesus tells us to drop whatever we're doing—even if it is the most sacred of things—and mend the fences of fellowship.

The second illustration involves an opponent in a legal dispute. Jesus' advice is to settle out of court as quickly as possible. In this case, as well as in the first, Jesus stresses the urgency of the situation and warns against letting wounded feelings fester (see Eph. 4:26b–27). The reason for such urgency is that we cannot be right with God until we are right with our fellow man (compare 1 John 2:9–11; 4:20).

The Relevance of the Truth

Although spoken two thousand years ago, these words of Jesus are as relevant today as they were then. And we see that the moral

---

5. Note that the relationship is with a "brother," which refers not simply to a family member but extends to someone close within the family of God.

precepts of the Law are not to be shed like molting skin but to be taken to heart and internalized. From our study today, three guidelines emerge.

First: *The principles of Scripture go deeper than externals.* If all you gain from church or from your religious activities is a surface kind of life, you're missing the heart of the Christian faith. It's like being married without being in love, like practicing law without a zeal for justice, or like preaching without a passion for truth (see Isa. 29:13).

Second: *The potential of anger is greater than words.* Words thrust in anger have a powerful force behind them that can be deadly. You can kill the spirit as easily with a sharp tongue as you can the body with a switchblade. Both are lethal weapons and must be handled with care (see Prov. 18:21).

Third: *The power of reconciliation is stronger than revenge.* A gentle word of reconciliation is far more disarming than hitting back to blacken the eye of the person who blackened yours. And when you reconcile yourself to someone you're at odds with, it's amazing what it does to your heart. It flushes out all the bad feelings that have collected there since the conflict began. You feel clean and free. No attorney can make you feel that way. Nor can any minister. The courage to restrain feelings of revenge and replace them with forgiveness must come from inside *you* (Eph. 4:31–32).

 Living Insights STUDY ONE

It was Bishop Ryle who eloquently distinguished the two testaments:

> "The Old Testament is the Gospel in the bud, the New Testament is the Gospel in full flower. The Old Testament is the Gospel in the blade; the New Testament is the Gospel in full ear."[6]

In what ways is the New Testament a fuller revelation than the Old (see Heb. 1:1–2)?

_____

_____

6. Bishop Ryle, quoted by John R. W. Stott in *The Message of the Sermon on the Mount (Matthew 5–7)*, rev. ed. of *Christian Counter-Culture*, The Bible Speaks Today series (1978; Downers Grove, Ill.: InterVarsity Press, n.d.), p. 71.

In what ways is it a more fragrant revelation (see Heb. 10:1–10)?

_____

_____

In what ways is it a more fruitful revelation (Heb. 8:6–13)?

_____

_____

🍇 *Living Insights* STUDY TWO

J. Oswald Sanders recounts a story about

> the great American preacher, Henry Ward Beecher,
> who was having constant trouble with the clock in
> his church. It was always either too fast or too slow.
> One day, in exasperation, he put a sign over it which
> read, 'Don't blame my hands, the trouble lies deeper.'[7]

Jesus hangs that same sign over Matthew 5:21–26, for the murder
done by our hands comes from the clockwork deep within our hearts.
What advice does the Bible have regarding the subject of anger?

Psalm 37:8 _____

_____

Proverbs 14:17 _____

_____

Proverbs 15:1, 18 _____

_____

Proverbs 16:32 _____

_____

---

7. J. Oswald Sanders, *For Believers Only,* reprint ed. of *Real Discipleship* (Grand Rapids,
Mich.: Zondervan Publishing House, 1972; Minneapolis, Minn.: Bethany Fellowship,
Dimension Books, 1976), p. 56.

Proverbs 17:14 _____

Proverbs 19:11 _____

Proverbs 22:24–25 _____

Proverbs 25:28 _____

Amos 1:11 _____

Galatians 5:19–21 _____

Ephesians 4:26–27 _____

Ephesians 4:31 _____

Titus 1:7 _____

James 1:19–20 _____

Is there any unresolved anger in your life? If so, toward whom is it directed? From the passages you just looked up, what should you do about that anger?

Chapter 5

SIMPLE INSTRUCTIONS
ON SERIOUS ISSUES

Matthew 5:27–37; 19:3, 7–8

With every newspaper that comes thudding onto your front porch, you have only to read a few pages over a cup of coffee before you begin asking yourself: Whatever happened to honesty?

Whatever happened to the George Washingtons who couldn't tell a lie to cover up the cherry trees they had cut down? Whatever happened to the honest Abes who walked for miles to return a few cents of incorrect change?

In the place of these exemplary statesmen, we have politicians whose campaign promises turn to pumpkins after the midnight of their inauguration. In their place we have public officials who go to any extent to cover up political charades and personal escapades. In their place we have Chappaquiddick, Watergate, the Savings and Loan scandal.

But the crisis in character doesn't stop with politics. It extends to touch even the most intimate of relationships—marriage. From Terre Haute to Hollywood, marital unfaithfulness sweeps across the country like wildfire. With each relationship that turns to ashes in the flame of misguided passion, we can't help but ask: Whatever happened to fidelity?

When partners cheat on each other and people lie to one another, the moral fabric of a nation frays and begins to unravel. But such things should not characterize those who have clothed themselves with Christ.

In this, His greatest sermon, Jesus addressed both of these serious issues—fidelity and honesty. As He did, He went deeper than the letter of the Law to divulge its spirit. With piercing simplicity, He made it clear that marriage requires absolute faithfulness and personal relationships require absolute truthfulness.

A Brief Reminder of the Sermon's Beginning

The Sermon on the Mount begins, appropriately, with the subject of character. With humility. With compassion. With purity.

With the character qualities necessary to impact the world as "salt" and "light." For it is in *being different* from the world that we *make a difference.*

In the balance of chapter 5, Jesus discusses the deepening of our walk with God, which is so necessary to bring about this change in character. With sobering incisiveness, He informs us that our righteousness must surpass that of the scribes and Pharisees (v. 20). For, although they were righteous on the outside, they were rotten on the inside (23:27–28). Their righteousness was all show and no substance (6:2, 5, 16). Their lips recited the right words, but their hearts reflected the wrong attitude (Mark 7:6).

Point by point in His mountaintop sermon, Jesus tells us that our decisions must be dictated by the deeper spirit of the Law rather than by the limitations of the letter. In doing so, He touches the true roots of murder and anger (Matt. 5:21–26), as we saw in our last lesson; and, as we will see today, marital fidelity (vv. 27–32) and verbal integrity (vv. 33–37).

A Clear Declaration of Two Absolutes

Unlike most preachers who tiptoe around explosive issues, Jesus walked resolutely through the mine fields of marital fidelity and verbal honesty.

Marital Fidelity

The shrapnel of dissatisfaction, disharmony, and divorce has struck marriages in every generation with devastating effects. When Jesus touched the sensitive subject of infidelity, He tried to disarm the common notion that confines adultery to a physical act.

> "You have heard that it was said, 'You shall not commit adultery'; but I say to you, that everyone who looks on a woman to lust for her has committed adultery with her already in his heart." (vv. 27–28)

In these verses Jesus bares the soul of the seventh commandment (Exod. 20:14), revealing that the source of sin is the human heart (also see Mark 7:14–23). By going to the heart of the issue, Jesus removed the gray areas related to adultery. His simple instructions introduced a then unheard-of question: unbridled lust equals adultery.

Now, when talking about sex, it's easy for the pendulum of popular opinion to swing to two extremes. One is Victorianism, which states that sex is shameful. But a person needs only to read the

Song of Solomon or Proverbs 5:15–19 to refute that theory. The other extreme is hedonism, which espouses a philosophy that all our sensual desires are to be gratified. But in these verses Jesus refutes that. Then, in the following verses, He goes a step further.

> "And if your right eye makes you stumble, tear it out, and throw it from you; for it is better for you that one of the parts of your body perish, than for your whole body to be thrown into hell. And if your right hand makes you stumble, cut it off, and throw it from you; for it is better for you that one of the parts of your body perish, than for your whole body to go into hell." (Matt. 5:29–30)

Serious words. But they merely echo the tone used by God in the Old Testament (see Lev. 20:10–16). Jesus took adultery seriously because it entangles rather than extricates. It creates confusion rather than resolution, and it impairs life rather than enhancing it.

The insidious intruder to the marriage relationship is not the alluring person on the outside of a home; it's the lust inside a spouse's heart. In the enigmatic verses of Matthew 5:29–30, Jesus advises that we should deal with lust decisively. He's not saying that we should literally pluck out our eyes or chop off our hands. Remember, the whole context of chapter 5 deals with going deeper than the surface, going to the heart of the matter. Jesus is saying that lust makes an inroad to our heart through the eye. Therefore, we should stop lust at the gate, using whatever measures necessary to turn it away. And since lust can be encouraged by the hand that touches another person, we should restrain ourselves there as well.

Issue of Divorce

The subject of adultery logically introduces a possible consequence —divorce. Jesus lived in a day when views about divorce were batted back and forth between rabbinic schools like a badminton birdie.

> Rabbi Shammai took a rigorist line, and taught from Deuteronomy 24:1 that the sole ground for divorce was some grave matrimonial offence, something evidently "unseemly" or "indecent." Rabbi Hillel, on the other hand, held a very lax view. . . . Hillel, arguing that the ground for divorce was something "unseemly," interpreted this term in the widest possible way to include a wife's most trivial offences. If

she proved to be an incompetent cook and burnt her husband's food, or if he lost interest in her because of her plain looks . . . , these things were "unseemly" and justified him in divorcing her.[1]

The Pharisees seemed to be attracted to Hillel's position and wanted to know which side of the net Jesus was on. That's what prompted them to ask the question in Matthew 19:3.

"Is it lawful for a man to divorce his wife for any cause at all?"

But whereas the Pharisees were preoccupied with the grounds of divorce, Jesus was preoccupied with the institution of marriage.

And He answered and said, "Have you not read, that He who created them from the beginning made them male and female, and said, 'For this cause a man shall leave his father and mother, and shall cleave to his wife; and the two shall become one flesh'? Consequently they are no longer two, but one flesh. What therefore God has joined together, let no man separate." (vv. 4–6)

The Pharisees volleyed back another question.

"Why then did Moses command to give her a certificate and divorce her?" (v. 7)

Notice that the Pharisees looked at the Mosaic provision as a *command*, but in verse 8, Jesus viewed it as merely a *concession*.

He said to them, "Because of your hardness of heart, Moses permitted you to divorce your wives; but from the beginning it has not been this way."

It's apparent that the Pharisees regarded divorce lightly. Jesus, however, took it seriously. But He does make a provision for the dissolution of the marriage bond in chapter 5, verses 31–32.

"And it was said, 'Whoever divorces his wife, let him give her a certificate of dismissal'; but I say to you that

1. John R. W. Stott, *The Message of the Sermon on the Mount (Matthew 5–7)*, rev. ed. of *Christian Counter-Culture*, The Bible Speaks Today series (1978; Downers Grove, Ill.: InterVarsity Press, n.d.), p. 93.

everyone who divorces his wife, except for the cause of unchastity, makes her commit adultery; and whoever marries a divorced woman commits adultery."

This exception clause states that grounds for divorce occur when there is a continuation of sexual intimacy with someone outside the marriage bond. Even so, divorce is not prescribed, only permitted.[2]

Verbal Integrity

The subject of divorce naturally takes us back to our wedding vows, where we promised to stay with our partner "for better or for worse." Maybe that's why the next topic in Christ's sermon deals with vows.

> "Again, you have heard that the ancients were told, 'You shall not make false vows, but shall fulfill your vows to the Lord.' But I say to you, make no oath at all, either by heaven, for it is the throne of God, or by the earth, for it is the footstool of His feet, or by Jerusalem, for it is the city of the great King. Nor shall you make an oath by your head, for you cannot make one hair white or black. But let your statement be, 'Yes, yes' or 'No, no'; and anything beyond these is of evil."[3] (vv. 33–37)

Oaths involve taking vows for the purpose of adding veracity to our statements. By doing so, we shore up our sagging credibility with promises. We used to do this when we were kids, remember? "Cross my heart and hope to die . . . I swear on a stack of Bibles!" We add these little oaths to buttress what we say because we're afraid people won't take our word at face value. Jesus' point is that our character should have so much credibility that the simplest of statements should be enough to guarantee our intentions.

A Personal Commitment to the Savior's Words

It's not enough to understand the Savior's words; we have to make a personal commitment to them. First of all, regarding fidelity,

---

2. The higher ground, of course, for the Christian is forgiveness and reconciliation (see 1 Cor. 13:5, 7; Eph. 4:31–32; Col. 3:12–13).

3. Or "of the Evil One."

we should marry for life or not marry at all. Second, regarding honesty, we should say what we mean or say nothing at all.

Whatever happened to fidelity and honesty? You will not find them touted in the tabloids or acclaimed on the airwaves. But if you'll take a look in the Sermon on the Mount, you'll find them alive and well and waiting for you to incorporate them into your life.

Isn't it time you took a hard look at these two important character qualities to see how central they are in your life? You may not be having a torrid affair or dispensing lies like a vending machine, but what if your heart was revealed for all to see? How would you feel about that? How would you feel about the lustful thoughts lurking in the back alleys? How would you feel about the cloaked deceptions loitering in the shadows?

 Living Insights

Helmut Thielicke once gave a series of messages on the Sermon on the Mount. In one of his sermons, the renowned German theologian came to a poignant conclusion that relates to our passage.

> Hermann Bezzel, the great preacher, quite rightly said, "White lies are silken threads that bind us to the Enemy, invisible webs that are woven in hell."
>
> True, they are "silken threads" which are not seen at first. In hell everything begins with little innocuous things. . . . A _murder_ begins with the slender, silken fibers of a few thoughts, quite internal, naturally, and well concealed in the precincts of the heart where thoughts have their privileged freedom and nobody can be forbidden to think. An _adultery_ begins with a glance. And the bonds of the greatest passions were once but silken threads. . . . So the delicate web of trivialities becomes a closely woven net of ropes in which the Accuser seeks to catch us and bring us as spoils to the Last Judgment.[4]

4. Helmut Thielicke, _Life Can Begin Again_, trans. John W. Doberstein (London, England: James Clarke and Co., 1963), pp. 57–58.

Describe how the following verses support Thielicke's conclusion.

Proverbs 5:1–6 _____

_____

_____

Proverbs 5:20–23 _____

_____

_____

Proverbs 6:27–33 _____

_____

_____

Proverbs 9:13–18 _____

_____

_____

How does the advice in Proverbs 4:23–27 parallel that found in Matthew 5:27–30?

_____

_____

_____

If the man in Proverbs 7:6–27 had heeded Solomon's counsel in Proverbs 4:23–27, at what point could he have been extricated from the adulteress's snare?

_____

_____

_____

Is there any relationship that is beginning to bind your heart with those silken threads that Thielicke spoke of? How enmeshed are your thoughts? How entangled are your emotions? If you're struggling with inappropriate feelings for another person, pray through Proverbs 5:15–23, personalizing it to your present situation.

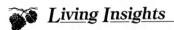

Living Insights

Besides Matthew 5:33–37, the Bible has a lot to say about the words we speak. Look up these passages and summarize their advice.

Proverbs 10:19 _____

_____

Proverbs 17:27–28 _____

_____

Matthew 12:36–37 _____

_____

James 1:19 _____

_____

What common thread of truth is woven through all these passages?

_____

_____

What advice does Solomon give to the person whose words have created a breach in a relationship (see Prov. 6:2–5)?

_____

_____

Spend a few minutes praying about the words that have come from your lips the past twenty-four hours. Are there any you wish you could take back? Any you need to pluck from your vocabulary? Any you need to apologize for? Do something about them right now, won't you?

Chapter 6

SIMPLE ADVICE
TO THE SELFISH
AND STRONG-WILLED

Matthew 5:38–48

Every generation, it seems, has its slogans. When America was struggling to win its independence, a number of slogans attracted national attention: Trust in God but Keep Your Powder Dry . . . Give Me Liberty or Give Me Death.

When the United States entered World War II, the slogan that echoed across the country was Remember Pearl Harbor! But the patriotic spirit that buoyed in the wake of that war sank in the sixties. Scrawled in spray paint on war memorials were the slogans of a generation adrift, a generation cut loose from the moorings of its ancestors: Turn On, Tune In, Drop Out . . . Don't Trust Anyone Over 30.

Absolutes eroded during the sixties and seventies, as did traditional values and the once hallowed institutions of home, marriage, and church. They were washed away by a tide of apathy.

When that tide ebbed, we, as a nation, took inventory of our losses and found that a spirit of selfishness was left, thus making the eighties the "Me Generation." The ad campaigns tapped into that spirit with a whole new series of slogans: You Deserve a Break Today . . . Master the Possibilities . . . Membership Has Its Privileges . . . Have It Your Way.

Our Dog-Eat-Dog Mentality

This widespread washout of Judeo-Christian values has created a different America than our ancestors fought and died for. America has become a melting pot of me-firsts, comprised of tired masses huddled around a handful of self-incriminating slogans: Do unto Others Before They Do unto You . . . Don't Get Mad, Get Even . . . Get All You Can, Can All You Get, and then Sit on the Can.

Ours is a selfish and volatile generation. If we became permissive in the sixties and disillusioned in the seventies, we've grown angry and defensive in the eighties and nineties. That "laid back" posture of twenty years ago has changed to a "fight back" one today. We have developed a dog-eat-dog mentality, and instead of domesticating the dog, we've unleashed it.

Christ's Countercultural Counsel

If we are ever to make an impact on our culture, we must not let ourselves become conformed to it (see Rom. 12:1–2). To avoid being squeezed into its mold, we must live counter to our culture. Jesus has been telling us how to do that in Matthew 5. In verse 38, He continues by referring to a long-standing code of conduct that His followers were called to live counter to.

> "You have heard that it was said, 'An eye for an eye, and a tooth for a tooth.' "

The origin of this law predates the Old Testament and goes back to the Code of Hammurabi. One article of this code states:

> "If a man has caused the loss of . . . [an] eye, his eye one shall cause to be lost. If he has shattered a . . . limb, one shall shatter his limb. . . . If he has made the tooth of a man . . . fall out, one shall make his tooth fall out."[1]

That law became incorporated into the legal framework of the Old Testament (Exod. 21:23–25; Lev. 24:19–20; Deut. 19:21). But the code of conduct for the subjects of Christ's kingdom goes beyond that. His followers are to release instead of resist (Matt. 5:39–42), love instead of hate (vv. 43–47), and be perfect, not merely human (v. 48).

Release Instead of Resist

To establish the foundational principles of His kingdom, Jesus dug deeper than the Code of Hammurabi, through the stratum of Old Testament legislation to the bedrock of character found in the Beatitudes. On the basis of that, He constructed *His* code of conduct.

> "But I say to you, do not resist him who is evil; but whoever slaps you on your right cheek, turn to him the other also. And if anyone wants to sue you, and

1. Quoted by William Barclay, *The Gospel of Matthew*, vol. 1, rev. ed., The Daily Study Bible series (Philadelphia, Pa.: Westminster Press, 1975), p. 163.

take your shirt, let him have your coat also. And whoever shall force you to go one mile, go with him two.
Give to him who asks of you, and do not turn away
from him who wants to borrow from you." (vv. 39–42)

Woven into these words are certain rights that we, in our human
nature, cling to: our rights to dignity, comfort, privacy, and possessions. When these rights become threatened, we hire the best legal
fists money can buy and litigate our way to winning them back.[2]
But Jesus' advice is that we take off our gloves and refuse the fight
in the first place. To be able to do that takes the courage to release
your rights.

Release your right to personal dignity. Note in verse 39 how carefully Christ chooses His words. He says, "slaps you on your . . .
cheek," not "punches you in the mouth." A "slap in the face" is
not to be understood literally but figuratively; it's a colloquialism
for an insult. And when insulted, the natural tendency is to strike
with a backhanded insult in return. But does that mean we are
never to defend ourselves? John Stott explains that Christ's prohibi-
tion is not against self-defense but rather revenge.

> Christ's illustrations are not to be taken as the charter
> for any unscrupulous tyrant, ruffian, beggar or thug.
> His purpose was to forbid revenge, not to encourage
> injustice, dishonesty or vice. . . . True love takes
> action to deter evil and to promote good. . . . He
> teaches not the irresponsibility which encourages
> evil but the forbearance which renounces revenge.[3]

Some have taken verse 39 to ridiculous extremes by promoting
passivity in every situation. Martin Luther cites one such example
of "the crazy saint who let the lice nibble at him and refused to kill
any of them on account of this text, maintaining that he had to
suffer and could not resist evil."[4]

2. As a point of clarification, Jesus is applying these principles to people not to nations.
He is not dictating a foreign policy; He is giving guidelines for His followers.

3. John R. W. Stott, *The Message of the Sermon on the Mount (Matthew 5–7)*, rev. ed. of
Christian Counter-Culture, The Bible Speaks Today series (1978; Downers Grove, Ill.: Inter-
Varsity Press, n.d.), p. 108.

4. Martin Luther, *The Sermon on the Mount and the Magnificat*, ed. Jaroslav Pelikan, vol. 21
of *Luther's Works* (St. Louis, Mo.: Concordia Publishing House, 1956), p. 110.

Release your right to cling to comforts. Verse 40 paints a picture of one who was in possession of a "shirt," or inner tunic, and a "coat," or outer cloak. This outer cloak doubled as a warm blanket. Under Mosaic law, it was a protected possession. It couldn't be wrested from its owner (see Exod. 22:26–27; Deut. 24:13). Jesus states, however, that His followers should even be willing to part with possessions they have a legal right to keep. For the benefit of Christ's kingdom and for the good of others, we should be willing to give up *all* our possessions—even the most basic of creature comforts.

Release your right to privacy and a selfish schedule. In Jesus' day it wasn't uncommon for citizens to feel the flat blade of a Roman spear on their shoulder and hear a command to carry some load.[5]

> If an official engaged on state business required assis-
> tance, he could conscript a passer-by into his service
> for the next stage of the journey. But the legal limit
> for such conscripted service was one mile. He had
> no power to demand further service.[6]

In verse 41 Jesus tells His followers that if they are to make an impact on their culture, they are not only to go the legal distance but to double it. To go the extra mile. To go above and beyond the call of duty.

Release your right to exclusive ownership. If God has allowed you to have something—whether it's a two-ton truck or a tiny hand tool—He expects you to share it (v. 42). Freely. Graciously. Unbegrudgingly.

In reference to this principle that Jesus espoused, commentator William Barclay asked a good question.

> Are we then to say that Jesus urged upon men
> what can only be called indiscriminate giving? The
> answer cannot be given without qualification. It is
> clear that the effect of the giving on the receiver
> must be taken into account. Giving must never be
> such as to encourage him in laziness and in shiftless-
> ness, for such giving can only hurt. But at the same

---

5. An example of this practice is when the Romans compelled Simon of Cyrene to carry Christ's cross (Matt. 27:32; Mark 15:21).

6. J. Oswald Sanders, *For Believers Only,* reprint ed. of *Real Discipleship* (Grand Rapids, Mich.: Zondervan Publishing House, 1972; Minneapolis, Minn.: Bethany Fellowship, Dimension Books, 1976), p. 79.

time it must be remembered that many people who say that they will only give through official channels, and who refuse to help personal cases, are frequently merely producing an excuse for not giving at all, and are removing the personal element from giving altogether.[7]

Love Instead of Hate

"You have heard that it was said, 'You shall love your neighbor, and hate your enemy.'" (v. 43)

The first half of verse 43 about loving your neighbor is taken from Leviticus 19:18. But the portion about hating your enemy is not found in the Scripture. It was a gross distortion of the Law, twisted by the manipulative, self-serving hands of the rabbis and Pharisees. Surely they were aware of Solomon's counsel in Proverbs 25:21:

If your enemy is hungry, give him food to eat;
And if he is thirsty, give him water to drink.

Obviously, the religious leaders of Jesus' day let their emotions get the better of them when it came to their enemies, choosing to hate them rather than show love.

In verses 44–47, however, Jesus reverses the traditional teaching about enemies. First, He states an underlying principle in verse 44.

"But I say to you, love your enemies, and pray for those who persecute you."

We're never told to love the evil they do, but to love *them*. True love sees beyond the treatment it receives. True love doesn't need agreement to proceed. True love prompts us to pray against all odds. But why are we to extend such love to our enemies? Verse 45a provides the answer.

"In order that you may be sons of your Father who is in heaven."

The words spoken by Jesus were Aramaic, which is closely akin to Hebrew. Both Semitic languages were not rich in adjectives. So instead of saying, "He is a peaceful man," a Hebrew would say, "He

7. Barclay, *The Gospel of Matthew*, vol. 1, p. 172.

is a son of peace." Instead of saying, "She is a godly woman," a Hebrew would say, "She is a daughter of God."

Consequently, the phrase "sons of your Father" should be interpreted as "Fatherlike" or "Godlike." How do we become *like* the Father? By emulating His example. Look at the last half of verse 45.

> "For He causes His sun to rise on the evil and the good, and sends rain on the righteous and the un-righteous."

He shares the warmth of the sun without partiality. He shares the life-giving rain without discrimination. He extends common grace to the righteous as well as the rebellious.

In verses 46–47, Jesus states that what separates us from the world is a superhuman love that extends beyond our friends and family to encompass even our foes.

> "For if you love those who love you, what reward have you? Do not even the tax-gatherers do the same? And if you greet your brothers only, what do you do more than others? Do not even the Gentiles do the same?"

Only God's love is so expansive. And if we are to become like Him, we need to love like that too.

Be "Perfect," Not Merely Human

The words of Alfred Plummer offer a gleam of insight into this passage.

> To return evil for good is devilish; to return good for good is human; to return good for evil is divine. To love as God loves is moral perfection, and this perfection Christ tells us to aim at.[8]

The word *perfect* in verse 48 is *teleios*. The Greek idea behind this word is functional rather than philosophical. If you are working on your boat trailer, for example, and need a particular size wrench, the one that fits—the one that does the job—is a "perfect" wrench. That is, it has fulfilled the purpose for which it was made.

---

8. Alfred Plummer, *An Exegetical Commentary on the Gospel According to S. Matthew* (London, England: Robert Scott, 1909), p. 89.

Similarly, we fulfill the purpose for which we were made when we love as God loves, with a love so prodigious that it stretches beyond the narrow boundaries of human love.

How May All This Be Applied?

Start with your relationship with your family, which is central to your relationships with others. Instead of clinging to your rights, release them. Be the first to give up your rights to the phone, the television, the weekend. Be unselfish. Start living for the good of the rest of your family instead of just for your own well-being.

Then move to the next concentric circle—your friends. Instead of keeping a running tab on their relational debts, look beyond their wrongs. Overlook the occasional breach of etiquette. Turn the other cheek to the insulting remark.

Finally, reach across the outer perimeter to where your enemies are camped. Fulfill your role by extending love to them. Be a blessing in their lives instead of a curse.

Will all this be easy? Don't count on it. You will probably encounter all kinds of misunderstanding and mistreatment. William Wilberforce did. When he began his crusade to free the slaves in England, his enemies slandered him, saying he was a cruel husband, a wife beater, and that he was secretly married to a slave.

Abraham Lincoln also met resistance at the hands of his opposition. When he took up the torch to free the slaves, he was treated with contempt and ultimately murdered.

In our lifetime, Martin Luther King picked up the torch of civil rights and advanced the cause of black people. But he, too, was slandered by his enemies, scorned, and later slain by an assassin's bullet.

Will loving your enemies be easy? History teaches us no. Will it be worth the effort? You bet it will. It may be a struggle, but that struggle will transform you. And when the angels look down from above, they will smile wistfully and say to one another, "She's the spitting image of her Father, isn't she?"

What a compliment. And what a way to make a Father proud.

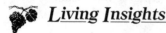 **Living Insights**

Let's put some teeth into today's study by personally applying what you've learned to your relationships with others, beginning with the inner circle of your family. Then in Study Two, we will travel through the concentric circles of our friends and, finally, our enemies.

What rights do you tend to cling to, in a self-centered way, where family members are concerned?

☐ Your dignity   ☐ Your privacy

☐ Your comfort   ☐ Your possessions

Which one of these rights do you cling to most tenaciously? Describe it in detail.

_____

_____

_____

_____

Why do you think you hold onto that one so tightly?

_____

_____

What effect would it have on your family if you released that right?

_____

_____

From Philippians 2:3–8, why should you release your rights (see also John 13:1–17)?

_____

_____

🍇 *Living Insights*   STUDY TWO

The second concentric circle we want to move into involves your relationship with your friends. Use the checklist from 1 Corinthians 13:4–8a to evaluate those relationships. For starters, pick only one of your friendships to run through the grid. Write that person's name in the following space.

With regard to _____ , I

- ☐ am patient.
- ☐ am kind.
- ☐ am not jealous.
- ☐ do not brag.
- ☐ am not arrogant.
- ☐ do not act unbecomingly.
- ☐ am not self-seeking.
- ☐ am not provoked.
- ☐ don't keep a record of wrongs done against me.
- ☐ don't rejoice when that person falls into sin.
- ☐ get excited about truth.
- ☐ bear that person's burdens.
- ☐ trust that person.
- ☐ am optimistic about that person's future.
- ☐ endure the strains of the relationship with grace.
- ☐ can always be depended upon by that person.

So, on a one-to-ten scale, how good are you at looking beyond that person's wrongs?

1   2   3   4   5   6   7   8   9   10

Describe the area that you struggle with most in this relationship.

_____

_____

_____

Now turn your attention to the outer circle of relationships where your enemies are camped. Name one enemy who particularly bothers you.

_____

How do you presently show love for that person?

_____

_____

What could you do that you're not doing now to show love for that enemy?

_____

_____

How often do you pray for him or her?

_____

When you do, what do you pray for?

_____

_____

What answers have you seen to those prayers?

_____

_____

How did Jesus respond to His enemies (see 1 Pet. 2:23)?

_____

_____

What did Jesus pray for regarding His enemies (Luke 23:34)?

_____

What effect does showing love to your enemies have on them (Prov. 25:21–22)?

_____

_____

Look up 2 Kings 6:8–23 to see an illustration of how Proverbs 25:21–22 works.

Chapter 7
BEWARE!
RELIGIOUS PERFORMANCE
NOW SHOWING
Matthew 6:1–8; Micah 6:6–8

E very preacher wears two hats—both of a priest and of a prophet. But this has not always been the case. Back in biblical days, priests and prophets had mutually exclusive roles.

The priest's work was routine. He studied the books of Moses, keeping their commandments and ceremonial requirements. His calendar was punctuated with the weekly routine of the Sabbath and the yearly schedule of feasts and festivals. He dealt primarily with externals: sacrifices . . . ceremonial washings . . . holy days . . . dietary regulations. His job was to preserve the past.

Not so the prophet. Unlike the priest, he was to interpret the present and give direction that would preserve the future. Every day on the job was different. Without rhythm. Without routine. Without ritual. What made it different was that he was called upon to interpret the daily news, which constantly put his career on the line. His courage and credibility were continually being challenged. He was not always wanted, was seldom respected, and if he did his job well, was often hated. Spontaneous emotion often took precedence over professional polish, in contrast to the priest. The prophet dealt primarily with internals, with the ethical erosion of the human heart.

Their respective roles could be summarized as follows: Priests calmed things down; prophets stirred things up. Warren Wiersbe tells us which job he would apply for.

> If I had my choice, I would rather be a priest than
> a prophet. . . .
> Most people don't want a prophet around be-
> cause [he] makes them feel uncomfortable. A prophet
> weeps while others are laughing, and a prophet wears
> a yoke that gets in people's way and knocks expen-
> sive trinkets off the shelves. . . . While the popular
> leaders bend with the wind, the prophet stands as

firm as a wall so he can lead the nation forward. . . .
He is a physician who exposes the ugly sores before
he applies the medicine. He is, in short, a person
who creates problems by revealing problems so that
he can solve problems.[1]

Before we turn our attention to the Sermon on the Mount, we
want to page back through the dusty annals of history to the words
of one such prophet, Micah.

Micah, the Prophet, Speaks

Characteristic of a prophet, Micah had delivered a scathing
indictment to the people (Mic. 3:9–12). His words had fallen on
the hearts of the people like hot irons. The searing rebuke raised
an important question: What does God require of His people?

> With what shall I come to the Lord
> And bow myself before the God on high?
> Shall I come to Him with burnt offerings,
> With yearling calves?
> Does the Lord take delight in thousands of rams,
> In ten thousand rivers of oil?
> Shall I present my first-born for my rebellious acts,
> The fruit of my body for the sin of my soul? (6:6–7)

What would be a sufficient enough offering to quench the white-
hot wrath of God? Several burnt offerings? How about yearling
calves that were worth much more? If not that, how about thou-
sands of rams? Or ten thousand rivers of oil? Would that be enough
to cool His anger? If not, would my firstborn suffice? My baby?

No! In place of all the complicated possibilities, Micah gives
one of the finest definitions of simple faith ever written.

> He has told you, O man, what is good;
> And what does the Lord require of you
> But to do justice, to love kindness,
> And to walk humbly with your God? (v. 8)

God is not looking for an external display or a public performance. He is looking for a simple faith that emanates from a heart

---

1. Warren W. Wiersbe, *The Integrity Crisis* (Nashville, Tenn.: Thomas Nelson Publishers,
Oliver-Nelson, 1988), pp. 61, 66–67.

of pure devotion to Him. The words of the prophet Micah form a fitting backdrop for the words of Jesus in Matthew 6.

Jesus, Our Lord, Instructs

In perfect prophetic form, Jesus begins chapter 6 with a warning.

Beware of This!

> "Beware of practicing your righteousness before men to be noticed by them; otherwise you have no reward with your Father who is in heaven." (v. 1)

This warning has to do with righteousness, an echoed reminder of what Jesus said earlier in 5:20. His focus here, like Micah's, is on our walk with God, our vertical rather than our horizontal relationships. He is speaking of our devotion to God, not our duty to humanity. His warning is to walk humbly, without pretext or pretension or pride.

But does this contradict what He said earlier about our need to shine our light before the world? John Stott clarifies this question for us.

> The fundamental warning Jesus issues is against *practising your piety before men in order to be seen by them*. At first sight these words appear to contradict the earlier command to "let your light shine before men, that they may see . . . ." In both verses he speaks of doing good works "before men" and in both the objective is stated, namely in order to be "seen" by them. But in the earlier case he commands it, while in the later one he prohibits it. How can this discrepancy be resolved? . . . The clue lies in the fact that Jesus is speaking against different sins. It is our human cowardice which made him say "Let your light shine before men," and our human vanity which made him tell us to beware of practising our piety before men. A. B. Bruce sums it up well when he writes that we are to "show when tempted to *hide*" and "hide when tempted to *show*." Our good works must be public so that our light shines; our religious devotions must be secret lest we boast about them.[2]

2. John R. W. Stott, *The Message of the Sermon on the Mount (Matthew 5–7)*, rev. ed. of *Christian Counter-Culture*, The Bible Speaks Today series (1978; Downers Grove, Ill.: Inter-Varsity Press, n.d.), pp. 126–27.

Having sounded the warning, Jesus now applies it to three cardinal works of piety: giving (vv. 2–4), praying (vv. 5–15), and fasting (vv. 16–18). Today's study will focus on the habits of giving and praying.

When You Give

Now the Prophet gets specific.

> "When therefore you give alms, do not sound a trumpet before you, as the hypocrites do in the synagogues and in the streets, that they may be honored by men. Truly I say to you, they have their reward in full." (v. 2)

Interestingly, the word translated "give alms" in verse 2 and the word translated "righteousness" in verse 1 are derived from the same Hebrew root. For the first-century Jews, helping the poor was synonymous with righteousness. But this pure act of righteousness became adulterated with the showmanship of the Pharisees.

The religious leaders put on a religious performance when they gave alms to the poor. As they walked toward the offering box in the synagogues, they were preceded by trumpeters who blew a fanfare. Then they carried the same ritual into the streets, seeking the public applause of men rather than the private approval of God (see also John 12:43). Jesus calls these grandstanders *hypocrites*.

> In classical Greek the *hupokritēs* was first an orator and then an actor. . . . Now in a theatre there is no harm or deceit in the actors playing their parts. It is an accepted convention. . . . The trouble with the religious hypocrite, on the other hand, is that he deliberately sets out to deceive people. He is like an actor in that he is pretending (so that what we are seeing is not the real person but a part, a mask, a disguise), yet he is quite unlike the actor in this respect: he takes some religious practice which is a real activity and he turns it into what it was never meant to be, namely a piece of make-believe, a theatrical display before an audience. And it is all done for applause.[3]

3. Stott, *Sermon on the Mount*, p. 129.

As verse 2 tells us how not to give, verses 3–4 tell how we should.

> "But when you give alms, do not let your left hand know what your right hand is doing that your alms may be in secret; and your Father who sees in secret will repay you."

These verses reveal several basics about giving. First, we should not become so conscious of it that we become enamored with our own generosity. Instead, our giving should be marked by spontaneity, not letting your left hand know what the right is doing. Second, we should give secretly and anonymously. And third, we should give with pure motives. Then our Father who sees in heaven will reward us, and that should be sufficient. That should be sufficient.

Some have argued, however, that seeking a heavenly reward for our earthly actions is mercenary, but C. S. Lewis diffuses that criticism.

> There are different kinds of reward. There is the reward which has no natural connexion with the things you do to earn it, and is quite foreign to the desires that ought to accompany those things. Money is not the natural reward of love; that is why we call a man mercenary if he marries a woman for the sake of her money. But marriage is the proper reward for a real lover, and he is not mercenary for desiring it. . . . The proper rewards are not simply tacked on to the activity for which they are given, but are the activity itself in consummation.[4]

What then is this reward from God? Is it a glittering jewel in our heavenly crown? Most likely, it is the inner delight that your gift has helped meet a need, that your life has made a difference in someone else's, that you have invested your money in eternity instead of squandering it in excessive self-absorption.

When You Pray

In verses 5–8, Jesus turns our attention to a second act of righteousness that is prone to being corrupted—prayer. Prayer was

---

4. C. S. Lewis, *The Weight of Glory* (New York, N.Y.: Macmillan Co., 1949), p. 2.

such a part of Jewish everyday life, it ran the risk of becoming ritualized, repetitive, and rotely exercised. So Jesus warns against performance, grandstanding for the gallery of pious peers. Keep in mind that He is not discouraging prayer but the wrong motives that lie hidden behind a mask of insincerity. As a safeguard against that, Jesus tells how not to pray.

> "And when you pray, you are not to be as the hypocrites; for they love to stand and pray in the synagogues and on the street corners, in order to be seen by men. Truly I say to you, they have their reward in full." (v. 5)

Note that the hypocrites don't love to pray; they love to be *seen* praying. They love the attention and garlands of praise that are thrown their way. Since they play to the audience, their reward is applause. But that's the extent of their reward. There will be no ovation for them in heaven.

In the verses that follow, Jesus tells us how we should pray.

> "But you, when you pray, go into your inner room, and when you have shut your door, pray to your Father who is in secret, and your Father who sees in secret will repay you." (v. 6)

First, we should go to a secret place and shut the door. There's nothing wrong with public prayer, but the reference here is to private devotion. Intimate contact with God should be discreet, not a stiff and empty routine on display. It should be spontaneous, filled with passion for God, the type of passion we find in the Psalms.[5]

> As the deer pants for the water brooks,
> So my soul pants for Thee, O God.
> My soul thirsts for God, for the living God.
> (42:1–2a)

> Whom have I in heaven but Thee?
> And besides Thee, I desire nothing on earth.
> (73:25)

---

5. For a contrast to this type of praying, see Luke 18:10–12, and circle how many times the words *I* and *to himself* are used. The person praying there is obviously absorbed not with God but with himself.

Back in Matthew 6, Jesus again tells us how not to pray.

"And when you are praying, do not use meaningless
repetition, as the Gentiles do, for they suppose that
they will be heard for their many words. Therefore
do not be like them; for your Father knows what you
need, before you ask Him." (vv. 7–8)

We should not use meaningless repetition nor should we model
the way the Pharisees did it. Long, eloquent prayers are not what
get the attention of God; simplicity and sincerity do.

And Now, the Spirit Applies . . .

Three principles emerge from the passage we studied today. First,
when devotion becomes a performance, we lapse into hypocrisy.
Second, when giving lacks secrecy, we lose our reward. And third,
when prayers are public demonstrations, we lack God's power.

Had Micah been there, listening to those principles, he would
certainly have been in the front row cheering—his "Amens" forming
exclamation points after every sentence Jesus spoke. For Jesus' words
were just another way of saying what Micah had said so many
centuries before: "Walk humbly with your God."

Living Insights   STUDY ONE

Before examining the specific deeds Christ addressed in today's
lesson, spend some time reflecting on your devotion to God.

How would you best describe it?

☐ intimate and passionate   ☐ lukewarm and dull

☐ warm but routine   ☐ cold and uncomfortable

Why has it been that way?

_____

_____

_____

What are some things that can quench your devotion for God?
Isaiah 59:2 _____

Luke 10:40–41 _____

1 Timothy 6:10 _____

James 4:4 _____

1 Peter 5:5 _____

1 John 4:20 _____

Are you doing anything that may be quenching the flames of your devotion?

_____

_____

_____

What could you do to fan the flames in your relationship with God?

_____

_____

_____

_____

 Living Insights   STUDY TWO

Helmut Thielicke once commented on Matthew 6:1.

> This cry "Beware," "Look out" reminds me of the warning calls I used to hear when we had to walk the dark, unlighted streets at night, when suddenly a trench or a stone or tangle of roots lay at my feet and I might have stumbled and fallen. The warning cry doubtless has the same meaning here. I can trip on a good deed, I can stumble over my Christian ethics and break my "spiritual" neck.[6]

---

6. Helmut Thielicke, *Life Can Begin Again*, trans. John W. Doberstein (London, England: James Clarke and Co., 1963), p. 81.

Our passage today warned us of two things we can trip over if we're not careful: our giving and our praying. Let's take a few minutes to shine a light on the way you do both. On a one-to-ten scale, from ostentatious to for God's eyes only, how would you describe the manner in which you give?

1   2   3   4   5   6   7   8   9   10

How do you feel when your giving is not recognized in some way by others?

_____

_____

Write a modern-day paraphrase of Matthew 23:3–7.

_____

_____

_____

_____

_____

Jot down anything from that passage that applies to you.

_____

_____

How does the way God sees us differ from the way others do (see 1 Sam. 16:7)?

_____

_____

What description best characterizes your prayer life?

☐ staged ostentation (v. 5)

☐ meaningless repetition (v. 6)

☐ guarded seclusion (v. 7)

Why do you think this is so?

_____

_____

What would it take to make prayer a more personal and mean-ingful experience in your life?

_____

_____

_____

_____

_____

_____

Chapter 8

PRAYER AND FASTING
MINUS ALL THE PIZZAZZ
Matthew 6:9–18

The enemy of our souls is an expert at pushing us to extremes. One extreme is fanaticism; the other, lethargy. It doesn't make any difference to Satan at which extreme we end up, as long as he can keep us teetering on the edge, far from the balanced Christian life.

Martyn Lloyd-Jones comments on the need to keep our balance and highlights one of the ways we often lose it.

> The Christian is to live in such a way that men look-
> ing at him, and seeing the quality of his life, will
> glorify God. He must always remember at the same
> time that he is not to do things in order that he may
> attract attention to himself. He must not desire to
> be seen of men, he is never to be self-conscious.
> But, clearly, this balance is a fine and delicate one;
> so often we tend to go to one extreme or the other.
> Christian people tend either to be guilty of great
> ostentation or else to become monks and hermits.
> As you look at the long story of the Christian Church
> throughout the centuries you will find this great con-
> flict has been going on. They have either been os-
> tentatious, or else they have been so afraid of self and
> self-glorification that they have segregated them-
> selves from the world.[1]

The extreme that Jesus addresses in today's passage is ostentation —making a public display of one's piety.

Brief Review: Give Anonymously, Pray Secretly

In Matthew 6:1, Jesus sounded a general warning regarding righteousness. He told us that we are not to turn our relationship with

---

1. D. Martyn Lloyd-Jones, *Studies in the Sermon on the Mount,* one-volume edition (Grand Rapids, Mich.: William B. Eerdmans Publishing Co., 1971), vol. 2, p. 13.

God into religious theatrics, because when we do, we get the credit reserved for God, and we miss the reward reserved for us.

In verses 2–8, Jesus got more specific. He said that when we give, we're to do it simply, sincerely, and secretly, knowing that our Father in heaven sees us and trusting that He will reward us (vv. 2–4). And when we pray, Jesus specified *where* we are to pray (vv. 5–6a), *to whom* we are to pray (v. 6b), and *how* we are to pray (vv. 7–8). We are to pray privately, to the Father, without meaningless repetition.[2]

Further Instruction: When Praying . . . When Fasting

Undoubtedly, the most famous prayer ever uttered is the Lord's Prayer, which is preserved for us in Matthew 6:9–13. Rarely does our Lord ever spell out the precise pattern to follow in any of the disciplines of piety. But here is an exception. What follows is a paradigm for prayer.

"Pray, Then, in This Way"

"Pray,[3] then, in this way:
  'Our Father who art in heaven,
  Hallowed be Thy name.
  Thy kingdom come.
  Thy will be done,
  On earth as it is in heaven.
  Give us this day our daily bread.
  And forgive us our debts, as we also have forgiven
      our debtors.
  And do not lead us into temptation, but deliver
      us from evil. For Thine is the kingdom, and
      the power, and the glory, forever. Amen.'"

As we take in the prayer as a whole, it's like taking in da Vinci's *Mona Lisa.* Standing before the famous painting, we are struck by

2. This doesn't mean that we shouldn't pray for things more than once, for Jesus prayed that way in Matthew 26:44 and taught others to do the same (Luke 18:1–7). What it does mean is that we shouldn't repeat the same words over and over in an empty recitation (compare Acts 19:34). The verb translated "meaningless repetition" is *battalogeō*, an onomatopoeic word similar to our word *babble*, which mimics the sound of meaningless chatter.

3. The implied *you* in the English version of verse 9 is emphatic in the original Greek. *You*—as opposed to the hypocrites and Gentiles—"*You* pray, then, in this way."

the power of her soft brown Mediterranean eyes, her ever-so-slight smile, her demure mystique. Like that old masterpiece, with its time-less beauty, its sublime strength, so this prayer hangs in Matthew's text. Framed in these few verses is the Son's portrait of His Father—His person, His name, His rule, His will.

The sovereign who is painted here is cross-cultural. So are the needs of His subjects—*give us bread* . . . *forgive us our debts* . . . *deliver us from evil*—needs that every generation of every land has had since the beginning of time.

Let's step up to verse 9 for a closer look at this picture. Jesus tells us how He would have us address God—"our Father." The words speak of a family relationship, a closeness, a respect, and the accessibility of a parent. Next, He tells us how we are to envision the Father—"who art in the heavens" (literally). Although He is as close as the air that surrounds us, He is as incomprehensible as the galaxies beyond us. Then He tells us how to regard Him— "hallowed be Thy name." His character is to be held in the highest respect, set apart from every other name that falls from our lips.

When we come to verse 10, we cross the border into the domain of His rulership. To ask that His kingdom "come" is to ask that it continue to grow, as well as to ask for its consummation. To request that His will be done is, in essence, to submit to it in our own lives.

His name. His rule. His will. How quickly we pass over these thoughts in prayer. How often we forget them altogether. But when we start our prayers by concentrating on Him, a certain perspective is gained, a respect is established, and authority is put in its proper place.

In verse 11, the emphasis shifts horizontally to "our daily bread." The reference is symbolic of the necessities of life, not the luxuries. The transition from bread to forgiveness in verse 12 is not as abrupt as it seems, for what bread is to our bodies, forgiveness is to our souls. It sustains us. Just as we need to pray daily for the needs of our bodies, so we need to pray daily for the needs of our souls.

The idea of asking God to forgive us "*as* we have also forgiven our debtors" is confusing at first glance. John Stott, however, gives a cogent explanation.

> This certainly does not mean that our forgiveness of
> others earns us the right to be forgiven. It is rather
> that God forgives only the penitent and that one of
> the chief evidences of true penitence is a forgiving
> spirit. Once our eyes have been opened to see the

enormity of our offence against God, the injuries which others have done to us appear by comparison extremely trifling. If, on the other hand, we have an exaggerated view of the offences of others, it proves that we have minimized our own.[4]

Refusing to forgive others can be a big temptation, which introduces the subject of verse 13. For many, this verse poses an enigma: To pray "lead us not into temptation" seems to imply that if we don't pray, He *will* lead us into temptation. Thus He becomes the one who solicits evil. Most likely, however, the verb "do not lead us" is a permissive imperative and could best be rendered, "Do not allow us to be led into temptation" or "Do not allow us to be overwhelmed by it to the extent that we are caught up in the snare of the evil one." The heart of the petition, then, is asking God to rescue us from the one who lies in wait, hungering for our souls (compare 1 Pet. 5:8).

Seventeenth-century Puritan Thomas Watson tells us why prayer for our rescue has such life-or-death urgency.

Satan envies man's happiness. To see a clod of dust so near to God, and himself, once a glorious angel, cast out of heavenly paradise, makes him pursue mankind with inveterate hatred.[5]

These three requests—for bread, for forgiveness, for deliverance—may also reveal a glimmer of the Trinity. For it is the Father who is our Sustainer, our source of daily bread. It is the Son who is our Savior, whose shed blood pays our debts. And it is the Spirit who is our Rescuer, indwelling us and leading us out of the darkness and into the light.

In the last half of verse 13 we find the conclusion to Christ's simple, profound prayer. Though the words "For Thine is the kingdom, and the power, and the glory, forever. Amen" are not in the earliest Greek manuscripts and probably not a part of Jesus' original prayer, the words capture the building drama of God's person and

---

4. John R. W. Stott, *The Message of the Sermon on the Mount (Matthew 5–7)*, rev. ed. of *Christian Counter-Culture*, The Bible Speaks Today series (1978; Downers Grove, Ill.: Inter-Varsity Press, n.d.), pp. 149–50.

5. Thomas Watson, quoted by Earl Palmer in *The Enormous Exception* (Waco, Tex.: Word Books, 1986), pp. 97–98.

radiance revealed. It is easy to see how these words might have been added as a passionate, concluding doxology.

However, instead of following His prayer with a crescendo of praise, Jesus gives a few sobering words of explanation to underscore the importance of forgiving others.

> "For if you forgive men for their transgressions, your heavenly Father will also forgive you. But if you do not forgive men, then your Father will not forgive your transgressions." (Matt. 6:14–15)

Here Jesus reemphasizes the all-important attitude of forgiving others if we hope to be forgiven ourselves. Two factors are necessary to make this transaction: first, the bedrock of God's grace to us, and second, the transfer of that same grace to others. Forgiveness essentially means providing others with the forgiveness in which we are able to stand. The intricately engineered structure of the Golden Gate Bridge illustrates this truth well.

> Its great south pier rests directly upon the fault zone of the San Andreas Fault. That bridge is an amazing structure of both flexibility and strength. It is built to sway some twenty feet at the center of its one-mile suspension span. The secret to its durability is its flexibility that enables this sway, but that is not all. By design, every part of the bridge—its concrete roadway, its steel railings, its cross beams—is inevitably related from one welded joint to the other up through the vast cable system to two great towers and two great land anchor piers. The towers bear most of the weight, and they are deeply imbedded into the rock foundation beneath the sea. In other words, the bridge is totally preoccupied with its foundation. This is its secret! Flexibility and foundation. In the Christian life, it is the forgiveness of the gospel that grants us our flexibility; and it is the Lord of the gospel who is our foundation.[6]

"And Whenever You Fast . . ."

The Lord changes subjects now, from praying to fasting, but the theme that threads its way through the passage remains the same: personal devotion to God should be expressed privately, not publicly.

6. Palmer, *The Enormous Exception*, p. 145.

"And whenever you fast, do not put on a gloomy face as the hypocrites do, for they neglect their appearance in order to be seen fasting by men. Truly I say to you, they have their reward in full. But you, when you fast, anoint your head, and wash your face so that you may not be seen fasting by men, but by your Father who is in secret; and your Father who sees in secret will repay you." (vv. 16–18).

Fasting was practiced for a multitude of reasons. Generally, it was practiced to deepen a person's devotion to God. But there were also some very specific reasons for fasting. There were, for example, certain compulsory fasts for Jews, like the one on the Day of Atonement (Lev. 16:29–34).[7] There were fasts associated with national repentance (Judg. 20:26; 1 Sam. 7:6; Neh. 9:1). Sometimes people fasted to intensify their quest for God (Dan. 9:3). And there were fasts to prepare a person to undergo temptation (Matt. 4:1–2).

Another reason, however, was not so honorable. It involved, once again, pizzazz to impress an audience. For it was not uncommon at that time for some who were fasting to leave their hair deliberately unkempt, to wear rumpled clothes, and even to apply cosmetic whiteness to their faces to accentuate the paleness of their skin color. Talk about theatrics! Talk about wearing masks! These hypocrites were not worshiping God; they were relishing an Academy Award-winning role! Theirs was not an act of devotion but of ostentation. The part they played was extreme.

But it was not the kind of fasting God desired among His followers.

Rather, when we fast God expects us to do it in the right way and with the right motives. Because even in our day fasting offers a variety of benefits. It is good for our health. It brings fresh perspective and helps us break old habits. It causes us to be more self-disciplined. And it simplifies life by bringing us back to the basics. But it was never meant to keep us from being healthy, happy people who enjoy all the benefits God brings to us (see Eccles. 2:24–25 and 1 Tim. 6:17).

7. "Although the Day of Atonement is frequently included in the calendar of Hebrew festivals, it was the most solemn day in the year and should therefore be regarded more properly as a fast. In Lev. 16:29 the Israelites were commanded to 'afflict themselves' on that day. . . . By the time of Isaiah (58:3–5) the idea of fasting seems to have been part of the observance." R. K. Harrison, *Numbers*, The Wycliffe Exegetical Commentary, gen. ed. Kenneth L. Barker (Chicago, Ill.: Moody Press, 1990), p. 370. See also Merrill F. Unger, *The New Unger's Bible Dictionary*, rev. ed. (Chicago, Ill.: Moody Press, 1988), p. 401.

An early rabbinic saying echoes this sentiment:

> A man will have to give an account on the judgment day for every good thing which he might have enjoyed, and did not.[8]

So in Matthew 6:17–18, Jesus is once again pleading for balance. He doesn't gravitate to extremes. He doesn't say to never fast; neither does He advise that fasting become a fanatical obsession. Do it, He says, but don't overdo it. Don't strut your spiritual stuff by making a parade out of something so personal and private.

Personal Obedience: How Can We Make It Happen?

Before we walk away from our passage, there are a couple of applicational steps we need to take.

First: *Make the heavenly Father, not people, your main focus.* Pray to our Father who art in heaven, not to all the people who art in the audience. It's *He* whose name is hallowed, not the people around us. It's *His* will that is to be done, not the sometimes improper expectations of our parents or our peers. It's *His* kingdom we are to pray for and to help build, not the kingdom of others.

Do you find yourself under the thumb of others' expectations and demands? Do you take your cues from those whose frowns of disapproval cloud your life? What do *they* know about God's will for your life? If you want to be set free from living under the measuring stick of some legalist, start focusing on God. Hallow *His* name. Build *His* kingdom. Do *His* will.

Second: *Make the secret place, not the public place, your primary platform.* Our devotion for the Lord is cultivated in seclusion, not on stage. If you're going to wear out some place with your presence, wear out your prayer closet. That's where convictions are forged. That's where courage is tempered. And, most importantly, that's where the Father wants you.

 Living Insights STUDY ONE

The Lord's Prayer reflects the multifaceted nature of our relationship with God. Go through the prayer and list the various ways in which we are related to Him.

---

8. Quoted by William Barclay, in *The Gospel of Matthew*, vol. 1, rev. ed., The Daily Study Bible series (Philadelphia, Pa.: Westminster Press, 1975), p. 236.

Prayer	Relationship Revealed
"Our Father who art in heaven,	*Child to father*
Hallowed be Thy name.	*Worshiper to God*
Thy kingdom come.	
Thy will be done,	
On earth as it is in heaven.	
Give us this day our daily bread.	
And forgive us our debts, as we also have forgiven our debtors.	
And do not lead us into temptation,	
but deliver us from evil."	

Now that you've discovered some different dimensions to your relationship with God, spend some time praying through the Lord's Prayer with a new freshness. Get away to a private place where you can say the prayer out loud, pausing over each line and thanking Him for specific things—as a child would thank a father or as a worshiper would thank God. Better yet, sing or hum the words as you pray.

 Living Insights

Fasting can take many forms besides simply abstaining from food for a prescribed period of time. For instance, you can fast from "Monday Night Football" or "L.A. Law" or "Designing Women." Or from television altogether.

Try it sometime.

Take out the listings and circle the shows you regularly watch. And yes, the nightly news counts too. So do religious broadcasts. Pick one or two shows and cut them out of your weekly viewing diet. During that time, get on your knees by yourself and pray. Cultivate a more personal, more private relationship with God.

You'll be glad you did.

And your Father who sees in secret will be too.

Chapter 9

WHEN SIMPLE FAITH ERODES
Matthew 6:19–24

Although our lives may now be melodious with God's praise, we can easily fall out of harmony with His will. Slowly, imperceptibly, our heartstrings can slip out of tune with God. When that happens, a cacophony of consequences follows. And those hearts that were once tuned to sing His praise will sound only discordant notes of regret.

The path of Christian service is strewn with the litter of disobedient disciples—disciples whose faith was once as sincere and alive as either yours or mine. But somehow their rocklike faith eroded, until nothing was left but a handful of haunting questions. "How could that possibly happen to him? He was always so strong," or "If she couldn't stick with her commitment to the Lord, how will I? I'm not nearly as mature in the faith as she was."

The Tragedy of Settling for Less

Defection doesn't happen overnight. Rather, each day brings us subtle opportunities to let up, to compromise. Nothing boisterous and bold, you understand, just little, secret things that wink at and flirt with us. The late Dr. Richard H. Seume had an eloquent description for those temptations: "the lure of the lesser loyalty."

Like erosion, which crumbles solid rock with small, patient bites, so the lure of lesser loyalties can crumble what was once a simple, solid faith. Solomon, for example, was seduced by his lusts (1 Kings 11:4); Gehazi, the servant of Elijah, was enticed by greed (2 Kings 5); and Demas was drawn away by his love for the world (2 Tim. 4:10).

Oswald Chambers sounds this sobering reminder:

> You have gone through the big crisis, now be alert over the least things; take into calculation the "retired sphere of the leasts."[1]

Some material for this lesson has been drawn from the chapter "The Lure of a Lesser Loyalty," from the book *Shoes for the Road* by Richard H. Seume (Chicago, Ill.: Moody Press, 1974).

1. Oswald Chambers, *My Utmost for His Highest* (Westwood, N.J.: Barbour and Co., 1963), p. 110.

Invariably, it is not the big things that entice us away from God. It's not the torrid affair or the grand theft. It's the little things that lead up to them—the lustful look, the envious heart. No matter how strong we are, we all have an Achilles' heel. We are all vulnerable, especially to the little things.

Little things begin in the heart. And no matter how grand our lives may look on the outside, God sees beneath our exterior to view those imperceptible things that lurk in our hearts (see 1 Sam. 16:7). He knows who we *really* are on the inside. His intent gaze never rests, searching the earth in order to support those whose hearts are completely His (2 Chron. 16:9). And what attracts His attention most are those pure acts of devotion done in secret, which no one else sees (Matt. 6:4, 6, 18).

With God, there is no distinction between our public life and our private life. All things are open and laid bare before Him (see Heb. 4:13). We can keep no secrets from God. Not even secret thoughts (see Ps. 139:1–4). This is important to understand, because it is in the secret realm that we first entertain temptation. It is there that we make the initial choices which will have such an erosive effect on our faith.

That's why Solomon warns us to watch over our hearts with the utmost diligence, for the heart is the source of the springs of life (Prov. 4:23). If we pollute that source, we taint all the streams that lead from it.

The Impossibility of Serving Two Masters

Matthew 6:19–24 speaks to this issue of loyalties and how they influence our heart using two illustrations: our treasure and our focus.

Our Treasure: What We Possess

"Do not lay up for yourselves treasures upon earth, where moth and rust destroy, and where thieves break in and steal. But lay up for yourselves treasures in heaven, where neither moth nor rust destroys, and where thieves do not break in or steal; for where your treasure is, there will your heart be also." (vv. 19–21)

In the preceding passage, Jesus discusses our possessions. The contrast He sets up is designed to help us decide which is better—our earthly possessions or our heavenly ones. One, He tells us, is ephemeral; the other, eternal.

It's important to understand that Jesus isn't prohibiting possessions in and of themselves. Scripture nowhere forbids the possession of private property. In fact, it encourages it so that we may provide both for ourselves and for those in need (1 Thess. 4:11–12; Eph. 4:28). Jesus also isn't prohibiting planning for the future. Scripture clearly teaches that the wise prepare for the days ahead (Prov. 6:6–11) and provide adequately for their families (1 Tim. 5:8). Furthermore, Jesus is not prohibiting pleasure in the things we own. As a matter of fact, Scripture exhorts us to enjoy the things God has provided for us (Eccles. 5:19; 1 Tim. 6:17).

What Jesus *is* denouncing is the selfish accumulation of things—living extravagantly to the exclusion of those in need. His focus is the heart (Matt. 6:21), that invisible realm which is a seedbed of garden-variety wickedness (15:17–20). Those who are lured by a lesser loyalty are first attracted here, in the hidden regions of the heart.

Take a minute to reflect on your possessions. The earthly ones must be protected, since they can be stolen, thus necessitating alarm systems and safe deposit boxes. Since some possessions can be destroyed by the foraging of insects and rodents, you need mothballs and rat poison. Since the elements can also do a number on your possessions, you need rust-proofing and fire-proofing. And don't forget insurance. Lots and lots of insurance. Home insurance. Car insurance. FDIC insurance.

Now take a look at your heavenly possessions. You don't need to worry, because you don't need locks on *those* doors. You don't need to diversify your portfolio to protect against inflation or deflation. And you don't need a dime of insurance. Those valuables are safe and secure, under lock and key of the Almighty.

In His mountain sermon Jesus is warning against the coveting of earthly possessions. His words are aimed at the miser and the materialist, not the everyday person who is working hard to make a living. Jesus is not denouncing need but greed.

Our Focus: What We Are

Turning from the subject of our treasure, Jesus now addresses the issue of our focus.

> "The lamp of the body is the eye; if therefore your eye is clear, your whole body will be full of light. But if your eye is bad, your whole body will be full of darkness. If therefore the light that is in you is darkness, how great is the darkness!" (6:22–23)

Just as the eye in our head affects the entire body, so our focus—whatever we set our hearts on—affects our whole life. Paul gives similar exhortations about focus in two of his letters.

> Set your mind on the things above, not on the things that are on earth. (Col. 3:2)

> Finally, brethren, whatever is true, whatever is honorable, whatever is right, whatever is pure, whatever is lovely, whatever is of good repute, if there is any excellence and if anything worthy of praise, let your mind dwell on these things. (Phil. 4:8)

Clearly, our minds determine the direction of our lives. Those who have fallen into some moral trap set by the enemy were first enticed because their focus was wrong. And ultimately, a wrong focus can trap us in a merciless bondage, enslaving us to the wrong master.

As long as we vacillate between loyalties, we are vulnerable to that bondage. That's why Jesus is so stern in His warning in verse 19. And that's why He says in verse 24:

> "No one can serve two masters; for either he will hate the one and love the other, or he will hold to one and despise the other. You cannot serve God and mammon."[2]

Because we live in an economy driven by voluntary employment rather than by slavery, it's difficult to understand the full impact of Christ's statement. You see, we *can* work equally well for two employers, but it would be impossible to serve two masters. Why? Because in a slave economy the slave was the sole possession of one master. Once that slave was purchased, his or her full allegiance belonged to the owner.

Martyn Lloyd-Jones reveals the real tragedy of serving the wrong master.

> According to our Lord here, these earthly, worldly things tend to become our god. We serve them; we love them. Our heart is captivated by them; we are at their service. What are they? They are the very

---

2. *Mammon* is the transliteration of an Aramaic word for "wealth."

things that God in His kindness has given man in order that they might be of service to him, and in order that he may enjoy life while he is in this world. . . . What a tragedy; he bows down and worships at the shrine of things that were meant to be at his service. Things that were meant to minister to him have become his master.[3]

Those who begin by choosing merely to lay up a few earthly treasures ultimately find themselves without any freedom of choice, hopelessly enslaved to the master of materialism.

The Security of Living in Truth

We need not go down the road that leads to enslavement. We can submit ourselves, instead, to Him who is the true way (John 14:6). The way of truth is a secure road to travel. For example, by living in truth, our options remain open. And our greatest source of truth is Scripture, whose light makes it easier to steer clear of a lot of snares. But when we walk away from the light and into the darkness, it's not so easy, and we're more vulnerable to stumbling and falling. The secret, of course, is making the right choices and making them day in and day out, because our walk with God is determined by those little decisions we make along the way.

Living in truth also keeps our focus clear. The secret here is serving the right Master. Keep asking yourself: Does this honor the Savior? Does this exalt His name? Does this bring glory to Him?

The tragedy of a message like this is to walk away thinking, "I don't have to worry. I'm on the right road with the wind at my back." Just remember, a wrong turn or two and you may end up like Robert Robinson.

Robert Robinson was born in England more than two hundred years ago. He lost his father at an early age, and his widowed mother sent the boy to London to learn a trade as a barber. There he came under the persuasive influence of George Whitefield, was soundly converted, and began at once to study for the ministry. At twenty-five he was called to the pastorate of the Baptist Church at Cambridge, where

3. D. Martyn Lloyd-Jones, *Studies in the Sermon on the Mount*, one-volume edition (Grand Rapids, Mich.: William B. Eerdmans Publishing Co., 1971), vol. 2, p. 103.

he became quite popular. This was the beginning of his lapse into careless ways and his eventual succumbing to [carnality].

We find him years later, traveling in anonymity in a stagecoach with a lady seated next to him who

was reading a little book with evident enjoyment. One page of that volume held special appeal to her, and she consulted it from time to time. Turning to her fellow passenger, a gentleman who, she presumed, was acquainted with the subject of religion, she held the open page toward him, and pointing to the hymn she had been reading, asked what he thought of it. The stranger looked at the first few lines.

> Come, Thou Fount of every blessing,
> Tune my heart to sing Thy grace;
> Streams of mercy, never ceasing,
> Call for songs of loudest praise.

The stranger read no further, but turned away, endeavoring to engage the lady's attention in something else. But she was not to be denied. Venturing another appeal, she told the man of the benefit she had received from the hymn, and expressed her admiration for its message. With that, overcome beyond the power of controlling his feelings, the stranger burst into tears. "Madam," he said, "I am the poor unhappy man who wrote that hymn many years ago, and I would give a thousand worlds, if I had them, to enjoy the feelings I then had.". . .

How ironic that, in the end of that hymn, Robinson seemed to prophesy his own zigzag course when he wrote,

> Prone to wander, Lord, I feel it,
> Prone to leave the God I love.

And so he did, and he died in defeat at the age of fifty-five![4]

---

4. Seume, *Shoes for the Road*, pp. 74–76.

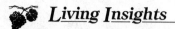

Lesser loyalties. They clamor for your attention like a crowd of Dickensian street urchins begging for pocket change. Once one of these lesser loyalties gets your attention, it vies for your devotion. Once it grabs that, it gets everything—your heart, your mind, your emotions, your time, your energy. It owns you—every bit of you— dreams and desires, thoughts and actions.

What are some of the lesser loyalties in your life that clamor for attention?

_____

_____

_____

_____

Which one has the firmest grasp upon your devotion?

_____

How does this distract you from your devotion to Christ?

_____

_____

_____

Study the account of Mary and Martha in Luke 10:38–42, and write down any insights you get that relate to your devotion to Christ.

_____

_____

_____

_____

Describe what went on in Martha's mind that got her distracted.

_____

_____

_____

How did her distraction affect her relationship with the Lord?

_____

_____

And with her sister?

_____

_____

List some of the things in your life that are "necessary."

_____

_____

_____

_____

Which is the only thing that is absolutely necessary, from Christ's point of view (v. 42)?

_____

_____

How does fellowship with Christ start (v. 42)?

_____

_____

Living Insights

Let's take a deeper look at one of the lures specifically mentioned in today's lesson—earthly treasures. In the parable of the soils, Jesus uses the image of thorns to describe how our spiritual vitality can be strangled and our growth stunted.

Name two "thorns" that choke out God's Word in our hearts (see Matt. 13:22).

1. _____

2. _____

Why is the thorn bush such an appropriate image for the Lord to use?

_____

_____

In what ways are riches deceitful?

_____

_____

_____

Have they ever deceived you? How?

_____

_____

_____

What can happen when riches become the focal point of life (see 1 Tim. 6:9–10)?

_____

_____

_____

How can you adjust that focus (see vv. 17–19)?

_____

_____

_____

_____

Chapter 10

THE SUBTLE ENEMY
OF SIMPLE FAITH

Matthew 6:25–34; Luke 10:38–42

In his excellent commentary *The Message of the Sermon on the Mount,* John Stott uses an illustration to reveal one of our society's many preoccupations.

> A few years ago I was sent a complimentary copy of *Accent,* a new glossy magazine whose full title was *Accent on good living.* It included enticing advertisements for champagne, cigarettes, food, clothing, antiques and carpets, together with the description of an esoteric weekend's shopping in Rome. There were articles on how to have a computer in your kitchen; how to win a luxury cabin cruiser or 100 twelve-bottle cases of Scotch whisky instead; and how 15 million women cannot be wrong about their cosmetic choices. We were then promised in the following month's issue alluring articles on Caribbean holidays, staying in bed, high fashion warm underwear and the delights of reindeer meat and snowberries. From beginning to end it concerned the welfare of the body and how to feed it, clothe it, warm it, cool it, refresh it, relax it, entertain it, titivate and titillate it.[1]

Caring for and catering to the body has become a national obsession. So much so that it has created its own set of anxieties: Are my clothes stylish enough? Is my home big enough? Is my portfolio diversified enough?

Enough, enough, enough. How much *is* enough? In our passage today, Jesus reveals this subtle enemy of simple faith. It's not anything as obvious as materialism or greed, anger, lust, or hypocrisy. No, it's much more secret, much more stealthy. It stalks your peace,

---

1. John R. W. Stott, *The Message of the Sermon on the Mount (Matthew 5–7),* rev. ed. of *Christian Counter-Culture* (1978; reprint, Downers Grove, Ill.: InterVarsity Press, n.d.), p. 161.

sneaks into your dreams, and slowly slips away with your simple faith. What is this insidious enemy? *Worry.*

A Brief Analysis of Worry

The term Matthew uses for worry, *anxious,* is used five times in Matthew 6:25–34. It comes from the Greek word *merimnaō,* which is a compound made up of two words, *merizō,* meaning "to divide," and *nous,* meaning "the mind." So literally, it means "to divide the mind." Luke 10:38–42 beautifully illustrates a divided mind in action.

> Now as they were traveling along, [Jesus] entered a certain village; and a woman named Martha welcomed Him into her home. And she had a sister called Mary, who moreover was listening to the Lord's word, seated at His feet. But Martha was distracted with all her preparations; and she came up to Him, and said, "Lord, do You not care that my sister has left me to do all the serving alone? Then tell her to help me." But the Lord answered and said to her, "Martha, Martha, you are worried and bothered about so many things; but only a few things are necessary, really only one, for Mary has chosen the good part, which shall not be taken away from her."

Jesus had stopped by His friends' home in Bethany for some simple relaxation and refreshment. But "simple" wasn't in Martha's cookbook. She couldn't serve the Savior a simple sandwich; she had to go all-out, preparing an elaborate meal. As she rifled through the kitchen cabinets, you can almost hear the questions bumping into themselves in her harried mind: *What shall I serve? On which set of dishes? How can I get it all done in time? Where's Mary?*

Whipped into a frenzy, Martha came frothing out of the kitchen. Verse 40 says she was "distracted." The word is *perispatō,* meaning "to draw around." It has the idea of being physically twisted around and mentally distracted.

What was the result of Martha's distraction? She blamed Jesus for monopolizing Mary and then instructed Him to tell her off! In replying to her, Jesus used that word again, *merimnaō:* "Martha, Martha, you are worried [*merimnaō*] and bothered about so many things" (v. 41). Her mind was divided and in a state of agitation. Her own simple faith had been sabotaged by a subtle enemy—worry.

What is worry? *Assuming responsibility for things that are useless, needless, or beyond your control.* What is wrong with it? It's incompatible with faith. Oftentimes, worry stems from unrealistic expectations. That was where Martha went wrong. She expected Jesus to be famished for food; but what He was starved for was fellowship—something that Mary recognized but that Martha completely overlooked.

Jesus' Counsel to Worriers

The final verses of Matthew 6 tie in beautifully with the previous section. Jesus has just been saying, "Don't lay up treasures on earth. . . . Don't fix your attention on the horizontal. . . . You cannot serve two masters at once." Essentially, He is saying, "Don't become enslaved to an earthly perspective." If you do, you'll become a worrier, living a distracted life that is preoccupied with all the "what-ifs." *What if we go to war? What if the economy goes into a recession? What if I lose my job? What if . . . what if . . . what if . . .* Jesus' antidote for anxiety is found in verses 25–32.

> "For this reason I say to you, do not be anxious for your life, as to what you shall eat, or what you shall drink; nor for your body, as to what you shall put on. Is not life more than food, and the body than clothing? Look at the birds of the air, that they do not sow, neither do they reap, nor gather into barns, and yet your heavenly Father feeds them. Are you not worth much more than they? And which of you by being anxious can add a single cubit to his life's span? And why are you anxious about clothing? Observe how the lilies of the field grow; they do not toil nor do they spin, yet I say to you that even Solomon in all his glory did not clothe himself like one of these. But if God so arrays the grass of the field, which is alive today and tomorrow is thrown into the furnace, will He not much more do so for you, O men of little faith? Do not be anxious then, saying, 'What shall we eat?' or 'What shall we drink?' or 'With what shall we clothe ourselves?' For all these things the Gentiles eagerly seek; for your heavenly Father knows that you need all these things."

Jesus' Repeated Commands

Twice in these verses Jesus commands us, "Do not be anxious" (vv. 25, 31). He closes with the same command in verse 34.

It's important to understand that Jesus is not promoting reckless neglect of responsibility or disregard for the future. What He is prohibiting is being obsessed to the point of distraction with things that are out of the realm either of our control or our responsibility. We are not to worry over the questions "What shall we eat? . . . What shall we drink? . . . What shall we wear?" We are not to become consumed over the next meal or the next fashion. As important as eating, drinking, and being clothed may be, they're not worth being "divided in the mind" to the point that they distract us from our devotion to Christ.

Neither are the issues of tomorrow worth the price that worry would have us pay today. Whether it's the big earthquake, the Great Depression, or global warming, the worries of the future are not important enough to mortgage away the present. In being preoccupied with tomorrow's problems, we think about everything that could possibly go wrong and fret about the odds of our being victimized. And what dies in the process? Hope. Worry siphons hope from our hearts—and hope is our main fuel for the future. So to keep hope alive, Jesus firmly warns us, "Do not be anxious."

Jesus' Penetrating Questions

Between verses 25–30, Jesus asks five questions that burrow into the depths of our souls.

1. Isn't life more than food, and the body than clothing? (v. 25)
2. Aren't you worth much more than birds? (v. 26)
3. Which of you by worrying can increase your height or your life span? (v. 27)
4. Why are you anxious about clothing? (v. 28)
5. Won't God do much more for you than He does for the grass? (v. 30)

These questions point back to vital foundational issues like temporal desires, worth, motives, and perspective. And Jesus underlines these issues through two vivid illustrations.

Jesus' Vivid Illustrations

When we get to the point of becoming preoccupied with obtaining food, Jesus tells us to look up at the birds of the air (v. 26).

They are God's natural preachers. Their song is a sermon of God's care. Their freedom in flight is an eloquent message of His provision. In using this illustration, Jesus argues from the lesser to the greater. If God provides food for the birds, how much more will He provide food for His very own children who are worth infinitely more to Him?

The second illustration Jesus uses is given in response to our anxieties about clothing needs (vv. 28, 30). He now turns our gaze away from the sky and onto the soil, where the lilies of the field bloom in regal resplendence. Again, the line of logic reasons from the lesser to the greater. If He so clothes the grass with such colorful attire, how much more will He make sure that we're provided for in this area?

Jesus' point in both illustrations is that God can be counted on to take care of His own. To worry over the things that are His responsibility is to doubt either His capacity to care or His ability to provide.

Jesus' Strong Conclusions

Jesus concludes His discourse on worry with a few words to the wise. First, *those who worry model the lifestyle of the pagan.* Worry is a way of life for them, and when we worry, we are adopting their lifestyle instead of a lifestyle of faith—"For all these things the Gentiles eagerly seek" (v. 32a). Second, *those who worry presume that God forgets*—"Your heavenly Father knows you need all these things" (v. 32b). With our worry, we make a tacit theological statement, that God is either unaware of our needs or unconcerned about them.

Our Relief from Worry

Worry need not keep you up nights, tossing and turning with a stomach tied in knots. You can get relief. How? Jesus gives us a two-fold prescription in verses 33–34. Let's open the cabinet of verse 33 to discover the first one.

> "But seek first His kingdom and His righteousness;
> and all these things shall be added to you."

First, we need a good dose of the right *priorities*. If we're going to get relief from the ulcer of anxiety, we've got to start rearranging our lives and putting first things first. That may be a hard pill to swallow, but that's what has to take place. *His* kingdom needs to be first—not ours. *His* desires need to be paramount—not ours. Both His kingdom and His righteousness are higher than any earthly needs we have. If the needs of heaven are number one, all of our earthly needs will automatically fall into proper perspective.

The second prescription Jesus dispenses is found on the next shelf in verse 34.

> "Therefore do not be anxious for tomorrow; for tomorrow will care for itself. Each day has enough trouble of its own."

The label on this bottle is *simplicity.* The directions read: *Stop living more than one day at a time.* Each day contains enough to be concerned about without overloading our mental circuits with tomorrow's problems. Our mental and emotional natures were designed in such a way that if we don't heed this advice, we can expect to blow a fuse and short-circuit our entire system. And what good will that do, either for us or for the kingdom of God?

Are you suffering from the subtle enemy of simple faith? Is your relationship with God riddled with the worries of the world? Are you so consumed with making a living that you've neglected making a life? If you're wringing your hands about what tomorrow may bring, maybe it's time you put those hands into the hands of Him who holds tomorrow. Look at the birds of the air. Look at the lilies of the field. And relax. If He has provided so well for them, how much more will He provide for you?

 Living Insights

The little worries that infest your mind scratch around like mice in an attic. They scamper around upstairs and distract you with their nocturnal activity. They nibble away at everything that is even remotely edible. And they multiply like crazy.

These little worries may seem harmless at first, but, like mice, they can eat away the electrical wiring in your attic. If you don't exterminate them, at the very least they'll distract you; at the worst, they'll destroy you.

What little mice do you have running around upstairs? What thoughts anxiously run through your mind?

What do you worry about most?

Why?

Have those mice caused any damage to the wiring in the attic? How has anxiety eaten away at your thought life?

One way to rid your mental attic of those destructive rodents of worry is by putting their natural enemy up there to chase them away. And that enemy is the Word of God. Put Philippians 4:6–7 up there and see if that doesn't send them scurrying away.

> Be anxious for nothing, but in everything by prayer
> and supplication with thanksgiving let your requests
> be made known to God. And the peace of God,
> which surpasses all comprehension, shall guard your
> hearts and your minds in Christ Jesus.

 Living Insights STUDY TWO

In today's lesson we peeked through the window into the kitchen of a well-kept home in Bethany. There we saw Martha distracted from her devotion to Jesus, in a dither over dinner. Has that ever happened to you? Probably a little bit every day, right? And sometimes a lot every day! Why not take a few moments to come out of the kitchen and quiet your heart. Philippians 4:6 advises the anxious to pray. If you struggle with anxiety, pray through the following prayer, quietly meditating on how it applies to your own life. Then continue praying about any specific worries that are bothering you.

Dear Savior at whose feet I now sit,

When you knock on the door to my heart, what is it you are looking for? What is it you want? Is it not to come in to dine with me? Is it not for fellowship?

And yet, so often, where do you find me? At your feet? No. In the kitchen. How many times have I become distracted and left you there . . . sitting . . . waiting . . . longing?

What is so important about my kitchenful of preparations that draws me away from you? How can they seem so trivial now and yet so urgent when I'm caught up in them?

Forgive me for being so much distracted by my preparations and so little attracted by your presence. For being so diligent in my duties and so negligent in my devotion. For being so quick to my feet and so slow to yours.

Help me to understand that it is an intimate moment you seek from me, not an elaborate meal.

Guard my heart this day from the many distractions that vie for my attention. And help me to fix my eyes on you. Not on my rank in the kingdom, as did the disciples. Not on the finer points of theology, as did the scribes. Not on the sins of others, as did the Pharisees. Not on a place of worship, as did the woman at the well. Not on the budget, as did Judas. But on you.

Bring me out of the kitchen, Lord. Bid me come to your feet. And there may I thrill to sit and adore you. . . .[2]

2. Ken Gire, *Intimate Moments with the Savior* (Grand Rapids, Mich.: Zondervan Publishing House, 1989), p. 69.

Chapter 11

IF YOU'RE SERIOUS ABOUT SIMPLE FAITH, STOP THIS!

Matthew 7:1–5; Galatians 6:1

Christians have a lot of indoor games they play. One of the more popular is Let's Label. Here's how it works. We find those who are different than we are—they may look different, sound different, think different, or act different—then we start the game, which is played in steps. First step: We find something about them we don't like. Second step: We examine the externals. Third step: We form critical opinions. Fourth step: We jump to inaccurate conclusions. Fifth step: We stick a label on them. Sixth step: We share our findings with others. The winner gets to wear a smugly superior look for the rest of the day.

There is another name for the Let's Label game. It's called *judging,* and it's wrong. Why is it so wrong? Because we are never able to know *all* the facts. Because we are never able to know *all* the hidden motives. And, because of these, we are never able to be completely free of prejudice. But most importantly, because such judging is disobeying the clear command of Christ.

Jesus' Timely and Relevant Counsel

That clear command is found in Matthew 7:1a, and it flashes out of the text like a neon sign.

"Do not judge."

Understanding the Command

The word *judge* is from the Greek word *krinō,* from which we get our word *critic.* The root meaning is "to separate," but it can also mean "to judge in a courtroom" or "to discern truth from error." To be able to judge truth from error is a mark of maturity and is not what Jesus is prohibiting. For proof of this, take a look at what He says in verse 6.

> "Do not give what is holy to dogs, and do not throw
> your pearls before swine, lest they trample them under
> their feet, and turn and tear you to pieces."

If you skip down to verse 15, you'll see that Jesus also uses discernment in exposing false prophets. Elsewhere, He *demands* that we make right judgments (see John 7:24). And if we turn to Paul's letters, we'll find that he, too, exhorts us to use discernment (see Gal. 1:6–9; Phil. 3:2). John, the closest to Jesus of the disciples, also echoes the Savior's thoughts in 1 John 4:1 when he tells us:

> Beloved, do not believe every spirit, but test the
> spirits to see whether they are from God; because
> many false prophets have gone out into the world.

Some judging, therefore, is not only acceptable, it is mandated. We are never expected to suspend our critical faculties or turn a blind eye to error.

Then what does Jesus mean in Matthew 7:1? Quite simply, He wants us to not be censorious, to not conduct our lives with a judgmental or negative attitude, to not assess others suspiciously, to not find petty faults or seek out periodic failures.

> When Jesus spoke like this, as so often in the Sermon
> on the Mount, he was using words and ideas which
> were quite familiar to the highest thoughts of the
> Jews. Many a time the Rabbis warned people against
> judging others. "He who judges his neighbour favour-
> ably," they said, "will be judged favourably by God."
> They laid it down that there were six great works
> which brought a man credit in this world and profit
> in the world to come—study, visiting the sick, hos-
> pitality, devotion in prayer, the education of chil-
> dren in the Law, and *thinking the best of other people.* [1]

When we pass judgment on others, we assume an omniscient role, suggesting that we are Lord and others are our servants. The Scriptures, however, specifically condemn this superior, condescending attitude.

> Who are you to judge the servant of another? To his
> own master he stands or falls; and stand he will, for
> the Lord is able to make him stand. . . . But you,
> why do you judge your brother? Or you again, why

1. William Barclay, *The Gospel of Matthew*, vol. 1, rev. ed., The Daily Study Bible series (Philadelphia, Pa.: Westminster Press, 1975), pp. 261–62.

do you regard your brother with contempt? For we shall all stand before the judgment seat of God. (Rom. 14:4, 10; see also 1 Cor. 4:4–5; James 4:11–12)

No human being is qualified to sit in that seat and pass judgment on others. Only Almighty God can do that.

Explaining the Reasons

Jesus next explains why we shouldn't judge.

"Do not judge lest you be judged. For in the way you judge, you will be judged; and by your standard of measure, it will be measured to you." (Matt. 7:1–2)

If we are harsh in meting out judgment to others, judgment will be harshly meted out to us in return. If, however, we are gracious and forgiving, we can expect to be treated that way ourselves, as Luke 6:36–38 affirms.

"Be merciful, just as your Father is merciful. And do not judge and you will not be judged; and do not condemn, and you will not be condemned; pardon, and you will be pardoned. Give, and it will be given to you; good measure, pressed down, shaken together, running over, they will pour into your lap. For by your standard of measure it will be measured to you in return." (see also James 2:13)

Following His concise command in Matthew 7:1 and His brief explanation in verses 1b–2, Jesus supports His point with a humorously exaggerated illustration.

"And why do you look at the speck that is in your brother's eye, but do not notice the log that is in your own eye?" (v. 3)

The Greek word for "speck" is *karphos*. It refers to a little, irritating particle, so tiny it's almost imperceptible. The Greek word for "log" is *dokos*, referring to a beam of timber. The contrast is bizarre enough to qualify as a *Far Side* cartoon!

Jesus doesn't say that it's wrong to help a brother or sister get a speck out of his or her eye. He does say, however, that it is inappropriate to attempt to do so when there's a plank stuck in your own. Jesus labels that person a hypocrite, a rebuke so strong that He used it in decrying the character of the Pharisees (Matt. 23:23, 25, 27, 29).

Everybody knows the tragic story of David's adulterous relationship with Bathsheba. Not as many know the story that followed. Rather than confess his moral failure, David attempted to cover it up. He called Bathsheba's husband, Uriah, from the battlefield and sent him home in hopes that he would sleep with his wife and thus think that *he* had been the one to get her pregnant. But the plan backfired. Uriah's loyalty as a soldier kept him from finding pleasure in the arms of his wife while the battle still raged. So to cover his adulterous tracks, David arranged for Uriah's murder. Months afterward, it seemed he had gotten away with that crime. Until the prophet Nathan confronted the king with a parable.

> Then the Lord sent Nathan to David. And he came to him, and said,
> "There were two men in one city, the one rich and the other poor.
> The rich man had a great many flocks and herds.
> But the poor man had nothing except one little ewe lamb
> Which he bought and nourished;
> And it grew up together with him and his children.
> It would eat of his bread and drink of his cup and lie in his bosom,
> And was like a daughter to him.
> Now a traveler came to the rich man,
> And he was unwilling to take from his own flock or his own herd,
> To prepare for the wayfarer who had come to him;
> Rather he took the poor man's ewe lamb and prepared it for the man who had come to him." (2 Sam. 12:1–4)

With the planks of adultery, murder, and deception sticking out of his eye, David passed judgment with fervor and conviction.

> Then David's anger burned greatly against the man, and he said to Nathan, "As the Lord lives, surely the man who has done this deserves to die. And he must make restitution for the lamb fourfold, because he did this thing and had no compassion." (vv. 5–6)

Nathan then took the wind out of David's pious sails when he informed him: "You are the man!" (v. 7a).

The words of Christ in Matthew 7:4 would fit David to a T.

> "Or how can you say to your brother, 'Let me take the speck out of your eye,' and behold, the log is in your own eye?"

Applying the Reproof

Many have erroneously concluded from this passage that we're not to interfere in other people's lives, that we're to mind our own business, to live and let live and leave the specks alone. But verse 5 refutes this position.

> "You hypocrite, first take the log out of your own eye, and then you will see clearly to take the speck out of your brother's eye."

Circle the words *first* and *then*. We have to get rid of the logs in our own eyes before we are qualified to retrieve the specks from the eyes of others. This idea is supported by Paul's counsel in Galatians 6:1.

> Brethren, even if a man is caught in any trespass, you who are spiritual, restore such a one in a spirit of gentleness. . . .

The word *restore* comes from the Greek word *katarizō*. It means "to put back in what's missing." The word is used for mending a net when fishing, for setting a broken bone, for equipping an army with food, for outfitting a fleet of ships for doing battle at sea.

Paul is saying, "You who are spiritual—who have removed the logs from your own eyes—*you* be the ones to be the agents of healing, you be the ones to set the broken bones, but with utmost tenderness and compassion."

The early church father Chrysostom added: "Correct him, but not as a foe, nor as an adversary exacting a penalty, but as a physician providing medicines."[2]

As you reach into that person's eye to remove the speck, remember several things. One, be sure your own hands—and heart—are clean. Two, specks in the eye are tender, so be sensitive and careful.

---

2. Quoted by John R. W. Stott in *The Message of the Sermon on the Mount (Matthew 5–7)*, rev. ed. of *Christian Counter-Culture* (1978; reprint, Downers Grove, Ill.: InterVarsity Press, n.d.), p. 180.

Three, you are dealing with a family member, a brother or sister in Christ. And four, you really don't know the strength of another's temptations.

A Few Suggestions for Conquering the Habit

Playing the Let's Label game is addictive; it is also destructive, both to the person who gets judged and to the person who does the judging. If we're not careful, judging can become so much a part of us that we're hardly aware we're doing it. Eventually, it becomes so distasteful a quality that people begin to distance themselves from us.

So how can we conquer such an entrenched habit? A step at a time.

First: Examine yourself before ever examining anyone else. Be more thorough with yourself than you are with others.

Second: Confess your own faults before confronting others with theirs. It will be easier for them to open up if you open up first. You will find that they will be only as open and honest with you as you are with them.

Third: Understand that person's struggles and be gentle in confronting. That's what Paul means in Galatians 6:1 when he says to restore "in a spirit of gentleness."

Fourth: Remember that the goal is restoration, not probation. The goal is not to prolong the pain of brokenness but to set the bone so that it will heal as soon as possible. That's the only way it will ever be useful again to the body—by being healed and restored. And once they are restored, we shouldn't belabor the sin that broke the bone. Nor should we stand looking over their shoulder to make sure they don't slip and fall again. Instead, we should put an arbor of affirmation around them and look to the road ahead.

In Conclusion

A final word about words. Be careful with them. Learn to be discreet in your conversations about your confrontations with others. Don't broadcast in public what's been confessed to you in private. Instead of hanging someone else's dirty laundry on the line for everyone to see, be sensitive to how that person would feel if you did, and only display what is clean and good about that person. It's just an extension of the Golden Rule, really—treating others the way you would want to be treated. And who knows, maybe some day the tables will be turned, and it will be your dirty laundry that people will want to see. Wouldn't it be nice then to have a friend who treated you sensitively and with respect and who could control his or her tongue?

 Living Insights

For a few minutes, let's take a look at the only person in the world ever qualified enough to pronounce a final verdict over a person's life—the Lord Jesus Christ. Let's look at Him in an emotionally charged scene where the scribes and Pharisees are attempting to manipulate Him into passing judgment on a woman caught in adultery.

First, read the account in John 8:1–11. Now describe the atmosphere of the scene.

_____

_____

_____

Articulate the attitude of the scribes and Pharisees.

_____

_____

Describe what you think were the feelings of the woman caught in adultery.

_____

_____

What do you think Jesus felt when He looked at the scribes and Pharisees with their hands filled with rocks?

_____

_____

_____

What do you think He felt when He saw the woman trembling in their midst?

_____

_____

What two things do we learn from verse 11 (see also John 1:17)?

1. _____

2. _____

Is there a broken individual in your life who needs someone to minister grace and truth to him or her rather than administer judgment? In light of Christ's example, what do you think that grace and truth should be?

_____

_____

Living Insights   STUDY TWO

For our next study, read through Romans 14. Woven throughout the verses in this chapter is the thread of judgment.

Have you ever passed judgment on someone who is a young Christian, weak in faith? If so, describe what you were critical about.

_____

_____

_____

The subject of Romans 14 deals with gray areas in the Christian life, not black-and-white issues like adultery, stealing, and so forth. Are there some gray areas that you tend to have a judgmental attitude about when you see other Christians involved in them? If so, jot down a few of them.

_____

_____

_____

From verses 3 and 10, what is the attitude we have to guard against in ourselves?

_____

What is the rationale for not passing judgment on another Christian's convictions (see vv. 10–12)?

_____

_____

What principles can you derive from this chapter about your relationships with Christians whose convictions differ from yours?

1. _____

2. _____

3. _____

4. _____

5. _____

Most often, judging others reveals our own insecurity, jealousy, and pride. When you're critical of others, what does it reveal about *your* life?

_____

_____

_____

_____

Of all the verses in Romans 14, which one is the Spirit of God using most to make an impression on something that needs changing in your life?

_____

Now take a few quiet minutes to pray through the passage, asking God to help you be more tolerant, humble, and accepting of other Christians.

Chapter 12

THE MOST POWERFUL OF
ALL FOUR-LETTER WORDS
Matthew 7:6–12

Colors fade, temples crumble, empires fall, but wise words endure through the centuries. And how beautiful is the well-crafted word that is perfectly molded to fit the particular circumstances in which it is set. As Solomon said:

> A word fitly spoken is like apples of gold in pictures of silver. (Prov. 25:11 KJV)

The most powerful of all words is a fitly spoken word, a *right* word that meets the precise need of the occasion. Mark Twain, a wordsmith himself, once wrote:

> The difference between the right word and almost the right word is the difference between lightning and lightning bug.[1]

And present-day wordsmith, Haddon Robinson, writes:

> There are bright words as brilliant as a tropic sunrise, and there are drab words as unattractive as an anemic woman. There are hard words that punch like a prize fighter and weak words as insipid as tea made with one dunk of a tea bag. There are pillow words that comfort people and steel-cold words that threaten them. Some words transplant a listener, at least for an instant, close to the courts of God, and other words send him to the gutter. We live by words, love by words, pray with words, and die for words. Joseph Conrad exaggerated only slightly when he declared, "Give me the right word and the right accent, and I will move the world!"[2]

---

1. Mark Twain, quoted by Haddon W. Robinson in *Biblical Preaching* (Grand Rapids, Mich.: Baker Book House, 1980), p. 176.

2. Robinson, *Biblical Preaching*, pp. 176–77.

In our passage for today, Matthew 7:6–12, Jesus handcrafts a few well-made words that create vivid images about dogs, pearls, pigs, and prayers—images that remain indelibly imprinted on our minds.

The Impact of Words Fitly Spoken

No one can fully measure the impact of words fitly spoken. Both testaments are a tribute to that fact.

From the Old Testament

Have you ever thought of the impact of two little words in the book of Genesis, spoken by Eve? She said to God, "I ate . . . ," and that forever changed the course of history.

Have you ever thought how the course of Abraham's life was changed when God told him, "Take your son . . ."? And when he was on Mount Moriah and Isaac his son asked about the sacrifice, Abraham replied with three words fitly spoken: "God will provide."

The book of Proverbs is a collection of words fitly spoken. Its author, Solomon, was not only a wise man, he was a wordsmith who forged words from the furnace of his heart, placing them on the anvil and hammering them into just the right size and shape to fit his purposes. In Ecclesiastes he tells us something of that process.

> In addition to being a wise man, the Preacher also taught the people knowledge; and he pondered, searched out and arranged many proverbs. The Preacher sought to find delightful words and to write words of truth correctly.
>
> The words of wise men are like goads, and masters of these collections are like well-driven nails; they are given by one Shepherd. (12:9–11)

The late J. B. Phillips once wrote:

> If . . . words are to enter men's hearts and bear fruit, they must be the right words shaped cunningly to pass men's defences and explode silently and effectually within their minds.[3]

3. J. B. Phillips, *Making Men Whole*, rev. ed. (London, England: Collins Clear-Type Press, Fontana Books, 1955) p. 75.

From the New Testament

Over in the New Testament we find the same stress on the value of words spoken fitly. Colossians 4:6 states:

> Let your speech always be with grace, seasoned, as it were, with salt, so that you may know how you should respond to each person.

James warns of the extreme volatility of words.

> And the tongue is a fire, the very world of iniquity; the tongue is set among our members as that which defiles the entire body, and sets on fire the course of our life, and is set on fire by hell. (3:6)

In His scathing denouncement of the corrupt religious leaders in Matthew 23, Jesus sharpens His words and wields them like weapons. He calls the scribes and Pharisees "hypocrites" (vv. 13, 15), "blind guides" (v. 16), "fools" (v. 17), "whitewashed tombs" (v. 27), "brood of vipers" (v. 33).

Much could be said about the words Jesus spoke. They could be called radical, controversial, idealistic, enigmatic. But they could never be called dull or drab. His words had an edge to them, which often cut both ways. In one swift swing of His tongue—"He who is without sin among you, let him be the first to throw a stone at her" (John 8:7)—He incriminated the adulterous woman's accusers.

It should be no surprise, then, when we come to the Sermon on the Mount, that the words of Christ cut a little sharply in places. Our passage today is one of those places.

The Power of Jesus' Penetrating Principles

The words we will be studying today have a strange ring to them. The One who urges us to take the Gospel to the ends of the earth warns us here against casting our pearls before swine. And He who warned us against judging others is the very One calling people names.

Dogs, Pearls, and Pigs

In Matthew 7:6 Jesus warns:

> "Do not give what is holy to dogs, and do not throw your pearls before swine, lest they trample them under their feet, and turn and tear you to pieces."

The tone of this verse seems to grate against the exhortation in the previous verses. John Stott explains this shift in tone.

> The context provides a healthy balance. If we are not to "judge" others, finding fault with them in a censorious, condemning or hypocritical way, we are not to ignore their faults either and pretend that everybody is the same. Both extremes are to be avoided. The saints are not judges, but "saints are not simpletons" either.[4]

Only simpletons would squander steak on stray dogs or a string of pearls on swine. To understand the full impact of these images, it's important to know that dogs and pigs were both unclean animals to the Jews. It would be unthinkable to offer consecrated meat from the sacrificial altar to wild dogs. Equally unthinkable would be to cast a handful of pearls into a pen full of pigs. Why? Because neither could appreciate the precious and priceless nature of what was set before them (compare Matt. 13:45–46). And the pigs, mistaking the pearls for peas, might become angered and turn to attack the one who cast them.

The illustration is most probably a reference to preaching the Gospel to those who might be either unappreciative of the priceless gift or angered by it.

> If people have had plenty of opportunity to hear the truth but do not respond to it, if they stubbornly turn their backs on Christ, if (in other words) they cast themselves in the role of "dogs" and "pigs," we are not to go on and on with them, for then we cheapen God's gospel by letting them trample it underfoot.[5]

Jesus practiced what He preached, applying the same principle when He sent out the Twelve on their first mission.

> "And whoever does not receive you, nor heed your words, as you go out of that house or that city, shake off the dust of your feet." (10:14)

4. John R. W. Stott, *The Message of the Sermon on the Mount (Matthew 5–7)*, rev. ed. of *Christian Counter-Culture* (1978; reprint, Downers Grove, Ill.: InterVarsity Press, n.d.), p. 180.

5. Stott, *Sermon on the Mount*, p. 183.

In Acts 13:44–49 and later in 18:5–6, we see Paul applying the same principle: *Discernment must temper our declaration of the Gospel.* What, then, do we do when those we love refuse the love offered them by God? What do we do when a hostile mate doesn't want to hear another word about Christ? What do we do about parents who want nothing to do with the newfound faith of one of their children? We pray.

Asking, Seeking, Knocking, and Receiving

From Matthew 7:6 logically flows the subject of prayer in verses 7–8.

> "Ask, and it shall be given to you; seek, and you shall find; knock, and it shall be opened to you. For everyone who asks receives, and he who seeks finds, and to him who knocks it shall be opened."

Notice the escalation of urgency in the commands found in verse 7: "Ask . . . seek . . . knock." Notice, too, that the verbs are present imperatives. Nowhere in Scripture are we chided for coming again and again to God in prayer. In fact, God encourages our coming to Him persistently, continually, and boldly (Luke 18:1–8; 1 Thess. 5:17; Heb. 4:16).

Which brings us to another principle: *Persistence must characterize our prayers.* So when it comes to prayer, don't be timid. Be persistent. And count on God to come through. Our Lord says as much when He promises that "it shall be given to you . . . you shall find . . . and it shall be opened to you" (Matt. 7:7).

Bread, Stones, Fish, and Snakes

Jesus concludes His remarks on prayer with a parable, a thumbnail sketch that illustrates a great spiritual truth.

> "Or what man is there among you, when his son shall ask him for a loaf, will give him a stone? Or if he shall ask for a fish, he will not give him a snake, will he? If you then, being evil, know how to give good gifts to your children, how much more shall your Father who is in heaven give what is good to those who ask Him!" (Matt. 7:9–11)

Jesus' desire is to explain how very trustworthy our heavenly Father is. Again, He reasons from the lesser to the greater. If an earthly father, being essentially evil and selfish in nature, freely gives his children what they ask for, how much more will our heavenly Father, being good and unselfish in His very nature, freely give to His children when they implore Him?

As you pray to this heavenly Father, it's important to keep two things in mind: first, God will answer our prayers in *His way;* second, He will answer them in *His time.* [6] But don't be discouraged; persistence pays!

Others and Us

In verse 12 of Matthew 7, Jesus shifts from our vertical relationship to our horizontal ones.

> "Therefore, however you want people to treat you,
> so treat them, for this is the Law and the Prophets."

To the surprise of some, this Golden Rule was not originally mined and smelted by Jesus.

> Much has been made by various commentators of the fact that the Golden Rule is found in a similar —but always negative—form elsewhere. Confucius, for example, is credited with having said, "Do not to others what you would not wish done to yourself;" and the Stoics had an almost identical maxim. In the Old Testament Apocrypha we find: "Do not do to anyone what you yourself would hate," and this, it seems, is what the famous Rabbi Hillel quoted in c. 20 BC when asked by a would-be proselyte to teach him the whole law while standing on one leg. His rival Rabbi Shammai had been unable or unwilling to answer, and had driven the enquirer away, but Rabbi Hillel said: "What is hateful to you, do not do to anyone else. This is the whole law; all the rest is only commentary." [7]

---

6. James gives two reasons why we don't receive what we want from the Father: One, we don't ask (James 4:2); two, we ask with the wrong motives (v. 3). Given the fact that we're asking with the *right* motives, we shouldn't stop asking, seeking, or knocking until we get an answer.

7. Stott, *Sermon on the Mount,* p. 190.

Although the mining of the Golden Rule wasn't original with Jesus, the refining of it was. He seems to have been the first to state it in a positive way. All others said, "Don't . . ."; He said "Do." This is no insignificant point, for the positive way of stating the rule focuses not on passivity but on activity. It puts us on the offensive, saying that our lives should be characterized by doing positive, helpful, merciful things for other people.

This leads us to another important principle: *Modeling must accompany our message.*

The Golden Rule espouses a principle so universal it can be used in virtually every one of life's situations. It calls us to put ourselves in the other person's shoes, to think to ourselves, "If I were there, how would I like to be treated?" Once we answer that question in our minds, we are to act on that answer.

It is no wonder Jesus concluded the Golden Rule, "for this is the Law and the Prophets," because it succinctly summarizes the spirit of Old Testament law. Words fitly spoken. Apples of gold in settings of silver.

Simply Put: The Greatest Message We Can Deliver

What is the greatest sermon we can preach? The one we preach with our lives—the message of Christlike character. Do you want to make an impact? Demonstrate the character of Christ. That's the distilled essence of the Gospel. Live as He lived. Love as He loved. Forgive as He forgave. Do as He did.

If you think that words fitly spoken are powerful, they are nothing compared to the power of a life fitly lived!

 Living Insights

Three principles emerge from our study of Matthew 7:6–12.

- Discernment must temper our declaration.

- Persistence must characterize our prayers.

- Modeling must accompany our message.

Take time now to try these principles on for size and see how well they fit your present lifestyle.

Discernment

How discerning are you when sharing your faith with others? Do you have the wisdom to know when to quit, the perception to know when your words are falling on deaf or defiant ears? Are you more prone to overstate your case or understate it?

_____

_____

_____

_____

What could you do to increase your awareness of situations so you'll become more in tune with how your audience is responding to your message (see James 1:19)?

_____

_____

_____

What are some things you can do when someone gets angry in a discussion about spiritual things?

Proverbs 12:18 _____

Proverbs 15:1 _____

Proverbs 17:14 _____

Proverbs 17:27 _____

Persistence

How persistent are you in your prayer life (see Luke 11:5–8; 18:1–8)? What is an example of something you've prayed about over a period of years that God has answered?

_____

_____

Did God answer your request exactly the way you prayed?

_____

_____

If not, how was His answer different?

_____

_____

What changes took place in your life or your relationship with the Lord as a result of those years of persistent prayer?

_____

_____

_____

_____

Modeling

There is a principle in writing called "Show, don't tell." It stems from a basic truism that showing is a more effective way of communicating than telling. It's the principle behind Jesus' words in Matthew 5:16.

> "Let your light shine before men in such a way that
> they may see your good works, and glorify your Father
> who is in heaven."

If you were suddenly struck dumb and couldn't communicate your faith by telling, what would people *see* in your life that would draw them to Christ? List five things.

1. _____

2. _____

3. _____

4. _____

5. _____

Living Insights   STUDY TWO

Let's take a closer look at the Golden Rule.

> "Therefore, however you want people to treat you,
> so treat them, for this is the Law and the Prophets."
> (Matt. 7:12)

List what you would want others to do for you.

1. _____
2. _____
3. _____
4. _____
5. _____

Now list how many of those things you do for others.

1. _____
2. _____
3. _____
4. _____
5. _____

How pure is the Golden Rule in your life?

☐ Solid Gold   ☐ 18 Karat   ☐ 10 Karat

☐ Gold Overlay   ☐ Fool's Gold

What one thing could you do today to start purifying that gold?

_____

_____

Chapter 13

SIMPLE YET SERIOUS WARNINGS FOR COMPLICATED TIMES

Matthew 7:13–23

It used to be that people enjoyed sitting back on a summer evening, relaxing on the porch swing and sipping lemonade, while high above frenzied moths swarmed around porch lights—zigging, zagging, looping, crashing into one another in a moth-eat-moth world.

Now we're the ones doing all the zigging and zagging. We're constantly on the move, flittering from one meeting to the next, always hurrying, looping, bumping past one another in a frantic race to get through overloaded schedules and complicated times. Probably if we slowed down long enough to look, it'd be the moths who would be sitting back, relaxing, shaking their antennae at our hysterical hurrying.

Busy. That's what life is like for many of us. Yet in the midst of all our frantic fluttering shines the calm, steady light of the Sermon on the Mount. Something about its insightful and relevant words attracts us. But the closer we get, the more we find ourselves beating our harried wings against white hot truth. We flutter around frenetically, bedazzled by its radiant light, but singed by the heat of our conviction and shame.

And the closer we get to Jesus' conclusion, the more intense the heat is that glares at us. For Jesus is not asking us to turn over a new leaf; He is asking us to be transformed. He's asking for a type of righteousness that surpasses that of the Pharisees, a type of righteousness that begins from inside our hearts and works its way out to consume every thought, every ambition, every emotion, every relationship.

A Strong Reproof

Jesus doesn't just tinker here and there with our lives. He doesn't suggest some minor, moral tune-up. He says we need a complete overhaul. We must either declare our allegiance to Him or decide *not* to follow Him; there's no middle ground. He puts these either/or decisions in front of us is in several sets of alternatives: two paths, two trees, two claims, and, as we'll see in our next lesson, two foundations.

Two Paths

> "Enter by the narrow gate; for the gate is wide, and the way is broad that leads to destruction, and many are those who enter by it. For the gate is small, and the way is narrow that leads to life, and few are those who find it." (Matt. 7:13–14)

Look at the contrasting adjectives in those two verses: narrow and wide, small and broad, few and many. How much more popular is the well-trodden way of the majority! What safety there is in numbers—what security.

In his autobiography, *Surprised by Joy*, C. S. Lewis pinpoints that time in his life when the wide gate and broad way attracted him. He was a schoolboy of thirteen.

> I was soon . . . "altering 'I believe' to 'one does feel.'"
> And oh, the relief of it! . . . From the tyrannous noon of revelation I passed into the cool evening of Higher Thought, where there was nothing to be obeyed, and nothing to be believed except what was either comforting or exciting.[1]

The broad way—where nothing must be obeyed and nothing must be believed—leads to destruction.

> There is a way which seems right to a man,
> But its end is the way of death. (Prov. 14:12)

The narrow way, on the other hand, leads to life. And that narrow way is Jesus Christ.

> "I am the door; if anyone enters through Me, he shall be saved, and shall go in and out, and find pasture." (John 10:9)

> Jesus said to him, "I am the way, and the truth, and the life; no one comes to the Father, but through Me." (14:6)

---

1. C. S. Lewis, *Surprised by Joy* (New York, N.Y.: Harcourt Brace Jovanovich, 1955), p. 60.

For there is one God, and one mediator also between
God and men, the man Christ Jesus. (1 Tim. 2:5)

Nothing is more unpopular than someone laying out narrow
roads for other people to follow. We don't like that. We like breath-
ing room. We like to stretch. We don't want someone crowding us.
And we don't like someone making dogmatic assertions. We like
opinion polls, surveys with multiple choices.

But Jesus isn't the type to hand out questionnaires to get a popular consensus on the issues. Do you know who does? False teachers
—the subject of the next few verses.

Two Trees

"Beware of the false prophets, who come to you in
sheep's clothing, but inwardly are ravenous wolves.
You will know them by their fruits. Grapes are not
gathered from thorn bushes, nor figs from thistles,
are they? Even so, every good tree bears good fruit;
but the bad tree bears bad fruit. A good tree cannot
produce bad fruit, nor can a bad tree produce good
fruit. Every tree that does not bear good fruit is cut
down and thrown into the fire. So then, you will
know them by their fruits." (Matt. 7:15–20)

These false teachers outwardly appear to be just one of the flock.
Inwardly, though, they are wolves. They are deceptive and danger-
ous. Their beauty is only fleece deep; their brutality runs much
deeper.

The more convincing the outer fleece, the more careful we need
to be in uncovering the inner character of a teacher. We need to
be careful not to be swept away by a teacher's charm or snowed
with his or her education. We need to scrutinize that résumé, no
matter how impressive. We need to be wary of this person's position
in the public eye, no matter how popular. We need to look beyond
the dross of ecclesiastical honors to find any cracks in character.
We need to look beyond the ribbons and bows of well-packaged
gifts of communication.

Then what? Then we listen to what is being said or left unsaid,
and we watch for the product being lived out.

In verse 16 Jesus changes from the analogy of what a sheep wears
to what a tree bears. Although we may not be able to see the wolf
beneath the fleece, there's no mistaking a tree—the type of fruit

it bears gives it away. Look at the fruit, Jesus is saying. If it bears apples, it's an apple tree. If it bears peaches, it's a peach tree. A wolf may be able to disguise itself, but a tree cannot.

A tree bears fruit *after its kind*. Fruit is a metaphor that includes the character and instruction of the teacher (see Gal. 5:22–23; Luke 6:43–45). And what is the standard by which we judge a teacher's character and teaching? The inerrant Word of God.

> The sixteenth-century reformers, who were accused by the Church of Rome of being innovators and false teachers, defended themselves by this doctrinal test. They appealed to Scripture and maintained that their teaching was not the introduction of something new but the recovery of something old, namely the original gospel of Christ and his apostles. It was rather the medieval Catholics who had departed from the faith into error. "Cling to the pure Word of God," cried Luther, for then you will be able to "recognize the judge" who is right. Calvin made the same emphasis: "All doctrines must be brought to the Word of God as the standard," for "in judging of false prophets the rule of faith (*i.e.* Scripture) holds the chief place."[2]

Two Claims

While Matthew 7:15–20 deals with false teachers, verses 21–23 deal with false followers—an equally unpopular subject.

> "Not everyone who says to Me, 'Lord, Lord,' will enter the kingdom of heaven; but he who does the will of My Father who is in heaven. Many will say to Me on that day, 'Lord, Lord, did we not prophesy in Your name, and in Your name cast out demons, and in Your name perform many miracles?' And then I will declare to them, 'I never knew you; depart from Me, you who practice lawlessness.'"

What is the problem in this person's life? What keeps this seemingly sincere, well-intentioned person from entering the gates of heaven? It is a reliance on credal affirmation or good deeds.

---

2. John R. W. Stott, *The Message of the Sermon on the Mount (Matthew 5–7)*, rev. ed. of *Christian Counter-Culture* (1978; reprint, Downers Grove, Ill.: InterVarsity Press, n.d.), p. 202.

What's so difficult in dealing with people like this is that all these things sound so right and seem so genuine. But the deficiency is not in what's seen or heard; it's in what is missing. What is heard is an intellectual assent, even an admission of Jesus' lordship. What is seen is a carrying out of His works under the auspices of dead religion, but in the name of faith. So what's missing? Just this. In everyday living, in the secret places of the heart, there is an absence of obedience. This is implied in verse 21, but it is spelled out in Luke 6:46.[3]

> "And why do you call Me, 'Lord, Lord,' and do
> not do what I say?"

A Personal Response

In this passionate and intense portion of His sermon, Jesus has issued three unpopular warnings:

1. *Only one gate leads to eternal life with God.*

2. *Only one kind of teacher deserves to be followed.*

3. *Only one kind of person can have assurance of eternal life with God.*

There's a three-point sermon during which nobody could doze off. It's a sermon with teeth that runs up and bites you in the seat of the pants. It sinks its canines in and doesn't let go! It can't help but get our attention. And it forces us to ask ourselves: Have I chosen the right way? Does my tree bear good fruit? Is the faith I claim evidenced in my deeds?

If the answer to these questions is no, you're lost. That's the simple, hard truth. And not a very pleasant one to hear. But it's better you hear it now than when you stand before the King, pleading, "Lord, Lord . . . ," and He says, "I never knew you; depart from Me."

 Living Insights STUDY ONE

According to Jesus, there are only *two ways*—easy and hard. There is no middle ground. They are entered by only *two gates*—

---

3. See also James 2:14–20. We are saved by faith alone, but the faith that saves does not remain alone. It bears fruit.

broad and narrow. There is no other gate. They are taken by *two crowds*—the many and the few. There is no neutral group. And they end at *two opposite destinations*—destruction and life. There is no third alternative.

It's time to do some sobering soul-searching with regard to the alternatives Jesus has set before us. Have you entered through that narrow gate? Are you one of the few and the forgiven? If you died tonight, would the road you're on lead you to life or to destruction?

The answers to those questions do not depend on your intellectual beliefs ("Lord, Lord . . ."). Neither do they depend on your good works ("Did we not prophesy in Your name, and in Your name cast out demons, and in Your name perform many miracles?"). The answers to these questions depend on whether you have knelt at the foot of the Cross and acknowledged your need for the Savior. That's all it takes, a simple, even halting step of faith—like the one taken by the thief on the cross: "Jesus, remember me when You come in Your kingdom!" (Luke 23:42).

And Jesus assured this man with the squandered life, "Truly I say to you, today you shall be with Me in Paradise" (v. 43).

 Living Insights

A survey we've done of our study guide readers indicates that most are churchgoing, born-again Christians. But there is always the chance that some are not. Could you be one of those people?

Maybe you are a very decent person, very diligent in your religious activities, but still very, very lost.

If you're not sure where you stand with the Savior, kneeling before Him is the best way to find out. We want to give you an opportunity to do just that by spending some time meditating on the Lord Jesus through the eyes of the thief crucified next to Him.

> We know nothing about that criminal on the cross next to Christ. We don't know how much he stole or how often. From whom or why. We know only that he was a thief—a wayward son over whom some mother's heart has been broken; over whom some father's hopes have been dashed.
>
> But we know one other thing.
>
> From Matthew's account, we know that he joined with the crowd in mocking Jesus:

"He saved others, but he can't save himself! He's the King of Israel! Let him come down now from the cross, and we will believe in him. He trusts in God. Let God rescue him now if he wants him, for he said, 'I am the Son of God.'" In the same way the robbers who were crucified with him also heaped insults on him.

"In the same way the robbers"—plural. They both joined in the sneering and taunting.

Question: What happens to change that one thief's heart—to give him the heroism to stand up for Jesus and the humility to submit to him?

Answer: He hears at arm's distance what Peter hears from afar and would write about years later:

When they hurled their insults at him, he did not retaliate; when he suffered, he made no threats. Instead, he entrusted himself to him who judges justly.

In the midst of the spears of abuse thrust into Jesus' side, this thief hears him appeal to a court higher than Caesar's. The appeal is not for justice but for mercy. And not mercy for himself but for his accusers. The spears are sharp and relentless, but Jesus does not throw them back. He bears them in his heart.

The one outlaw hears all this and lifts his faint head to look at the man from whose lips these tender words came. And when his eyes meet the Savior's, for a moment all time stands still. In those eyes he sees no hatred, no scorn, no judgment. He sees only one thing—forgiveness.

Then he knows. He is face to face with a dying God.

That thief didn't know much theology. He only knew three things: that Jesus was a king, that his kingdom was not of this world, and that this king had the power to bring even the most unworthy into his kingdom.

But we know one other thing.

And, in an intimate moment with the Savior, a lifetime of moral debt is cancelled.

Incredible, when you think of it. Amidst the humiliating abuse of the crowd and the excruciating pain of the cross, Jesus was still about his Father's business. Even with his eyes sinking on the feverish horizon of death, he was telling a common thief about the uncommon riches of heaven.

◆

Dear Jesus,

Help me to look at you through the eyes of that thief on the cross. And grant me the grace, I pray, to see in your eyes the forgiveness that he saw.

For I, too, have stolen much. When I have gossiped, I have taken from another's reputation, and in the process, robbed from my own. When I have raised my voice in anger, I have taken something away from peace. When I have aided and abetted immoral thoughts, I have stolen from another's dignity, depreciating that person from a sacred object of your love to a common object of my own lust. When I have hurt someone's feelings, I have taken something from that person's self-worth—something which might never be replaced, something for which I might never be able to make restitution. When I have spoken the truth, but not in love, I have stolen from your kingdom by pushing a soul, not closer, but farther away from the borders of paradise.

Remember me, O King, a common thief.

I stand before you naked in the shame of a squandered life—and I ask you to clothe me. I stand before you with a gnawing hunger in my soul—and I ask you to feed me. I stand before you thirsting for forgiveness—and I ask you to touch but a drop of your tender mercies to my parched lips.

Grant me the grace to live such a life that when you do remember me in your kingdom, O Lord, you may remember me with a smile, and look forward to the day when I, too, will be with you in paradise. . . .[4]

4. Ken Gire, *Intimate Moments with the Savior* (Grand Rapids, Mich.: Zondervan Publishing House, 1989), pp. 107–10.

Chapter 14

THE SIMPLE SECRET
OF AN UNSINKABLE LIFE

Matthew 7:24–29

 Tell me a story."

How many of you as kids crawled up on your father's or grand-father's lap and begged for a story to transport you from the drab present to some exciting moment in the magical past?

How many of you pored over dog-eared books by a cozy dormer window as rain pelted against the panes on a lazy Saturday afternoon?

How many of you dreamed of slaying dragons, discovering trea-sure, rescuing damsels in distress, or waiting for a knight in shining armor?

How many of you still yearn to skip down the Yellow Brick Road of Oz, fly away to Never-Never Land, or be asked to the ball by some handsome prince?

Stories. They have a way of staying with us, don't they?

Stories That Stay with Us

What is it that makes a story stick with us? Why is it that we quickly forget most of the information that goes in our ears but remember all of the great stories that enter our imaginations? There are at least three reasons.

First: *Because of the people and personalities that give a story interest.* We may forget the abstract concepts or the details of the places where the story took place, but the people and their personalities remain indelibly penned in our minds.

Second: *Because of their life situations, which we can easily imagine or with which we can even identify.* Frequently, the plot revolves around a mystery or struggle that holds our attention. As we follow the char-acters through the labyrinth of the plot, the decisions they make or the questions that are raised make the story memorable for us.

Third: *Because of their timeless lessons, which linger long after the stories are over.* From the explicit moral in Aesop's "The Tortoise and the Hare" to the implied moral in *To Kill a Mockingbird*, the lessons that subliminally seep through stories into our subconscious have an impact that's unforgettable.

Jesus was a master storyteller. His favorite form was the parable —an imaginary story with a real-life message. From the parable of the soils (Matt. 13) to that of the prodigal son (Luke 15), Jesus' stories still stick in our minds.

Sermons that stick also include a story or two that drive home a certain point. So it should come as no surprise that that's exactly how Jesus concludes His Sermon on the Mount. Did it work? Just look at the people's response:

> The result was that when Jesus had finished these words, the multitudes were amazed at His teaching; for He was teaching them as one having authority, and not as their scribes. (Matt. 7:28–29)

Let's look at this parable that had such a lasting impact on Jesus' listeners.

A Parable of Lasting Value

With His vivid imagery, Jesus' story bursts into our mind's eye like the winds that burst upon those two rain-soaked houses.

> "Therefore everyone who hears these words of Mine, and acts upon them, may be compared to a wise man, who built his house upon the rock. And the rain descended, and the floods came, and the winds blew, and burst against that house; and yet it did not fall, for it had been founded upon the rock. And everyone who hears these words of Mine, and does not act upon them, will be like a foolish man, who built his house upon the sand. And the rain descended, and the floods came, and the winds blew, and burst against that house; and it fell, and great was its fall." (vv. 24–27)

Identical Elements

Though they aren't given actual names, this parable has two distinct people doing identical activities. First, the two main people are both builders (vv. 24, 26). A closer look at the story reveals that Jesus isn't using houses and sand and rock in a literal way but in a figurative sense. He is talking about building a philosophy of life, establishing values, and making decisions that relate to life in general.

The second identical element in the parable is the life situation of each builder. Both face a storm of rain and winds and floods (vv. 25, 27). Again, the storm is to be taken not literally but metaphorically. Jesus isn't telling us how to stormproof our homes from Hurricane Hugo. He's telling us how to stormproof our lives. He's giving us blueprints for building lives that can withstand the calamities He sees looming on the horizon of our future.

Contrasting Factors

Although both builders do the same work and face identical storms, there are some significant differences between them. The first builder "hears . . . and acts upon" the words of Jesus (v. 24), but the second, though he "hears" the same words, "does not act upon them" (v. 26).

Interestingly, if we had seen the two buildings going up at the same time, we would have thought they were identical. But the test of the storm revealed their difference. You see, what's really important in life is not what we hear; it's what we *do* with what we hear.

The second contrast is in the ultimate outcomes of the two houses. The first builder's house "did not fall," even though the storm raged against it (v. 25). Consequently, the builder is labeled as *wise*. However, the second builder's house not only "fell," but "great was its fall" (v. 27). As a result, its builder is classified as *foolish*.

It takes no theologian to realize that the rocklike foundation of the wise man's house was Christ Himself; that builder had turned to Him in simple faith and actively built his life on Jesus' sure and eternal principles. The foolish man, however, disregarded Christ and constructed his life on the ever-shifting, ephemeral sands of this world's passing wisdom.

Years ago a severe storm blew across the life of Dr. Joseph Parker —a storm that came perilously close to washing out his life.

> Dr. Joseph Parker of London, the noted English preacher, who for many years proclaimed the Word of God in the great City Temple, tells in his autobiography that there was a time when he gave too much attention to the modern theories of his day. Men were reasoning and speculating and undervaluing the Word of God, and he found himself, as he read their books and mingled in their meetings, losing his grip intellectually upon the great fundamental doctrine of salvation alone through the atoning

blood of the Lord Jesus Christ. But he tells us that there came into his life the most awful sorrow that he ever had to bear. His devoted wife, whom he loved so tenderly, was stricken, and in a few short hours was snatched away from him. He was unable to share his grief with others, and walking through those empty rooms of his home with a breaking heart, his misery felt for some footing in modern theory and there was none. "And then," he said, addressing a company of his Congregational brethren, "my brethren, in those hours of darkness, in those hours of my soul's anguish, when filled with doubt and trembling in fear, I bethought myself of the old gospel of redemption alone through the blood of Christ, the gospel that I had preached in those earlier days, and I put my foot down on that, and, my brethren, I found firm standing. I stand there today, and I shall die resting upon that blessed glorious truth of salvation alone through the precious blood of Christ."[1]

Underlying Principles

Two principles run through Jesus' parable like strong, structural beams under the flooring of a house. First, *if you're only hearing the truth, you're not prepared for life's storms.* You can listen to hurricane warnings on the radio all you want and know what to do, but unless you get up off your couch and *do* something, you're going to get blown away.

Second, *if your foundation is sure, no storm will cause your life to collapse.* No matter how severe the storm, you *can* weather it if you've built your life on a firm foundation. No matter whether that storm is a tragic accident, the death of a loved one, a sudden financial reversal, or an assault by an enemy; you *can* make it through the storm. When the rain stops and the sun parts the clouds, you'll be there, still standing.

And So? Putting Yourself in the Story

The great sermon Jesus preached has not been preserved simply because it is a literary masterpiece. It is here to be acted upon. We are to step into it, make its truths our own, and, in doing so, dis-

---

1. As told by James Montgomery Boice in *The Parables of Jesus* (Chicago, Ill.: Moody Press, 1983), pp. 127–28.

cover the simple secret of an unsinkable life. It is building on the right foundation . . . the solid rock of Christ, rather than the sinking sands of a self-made life.

So now it's time to ask yourself a couple of soul-searching questions. The questions are not "Am I building?" or "Will a storm hit someday?" Both of those answers are clear. You *are* building whether you know it or not. And a storm *will* hit whether you're ready or not. And so?

And so you need to rephrase the questions. First, *Is the foundation you're laying absolutely solid?* You don't need a degree in engineering to answer that. Just take a good look. But not at all the self-help books on the shelf or the seminar notes in your binders. Don't look there. Look at your life. Look at what you're *doing* about what you're hearing. Second, *Is the house you're building eternally reliable?* Will life's storms level it? Can you say with confidence that there is nothing that will make it collapse? Are you laying a foundation that will allow you to ride out *any* storm, no matter how torrential?

It is our prayer that you will not only lay the right foundation but also continue on to build a life that displays all of the righteous features the carpenter from Galilee so carefully blueprinted in His Sermon on the Mount. Are you ready? It's up to you now, to act, to start construction today on the only life worth living, a life of simple faith!

 ## Living Insights

Before you add on any more rooms to your life or paint its exterior, let's send a building inspector over to take a look at the foundation. He's going to scrutinize it with a flashlight. He's going to be scratching notes on that clipboard of his to see if your life is up to code. And he's going to be asking you a few questions to see if you're *doing* anything about what you hear.

What was the last self-help book you read?

_____

What were a few things you learned from it?

_____

_____

_____

Of those things, how many have you acted upon?

_____

_____

Try to remember last Sunday's sermon. What was it about?

_____

How did you apply that sermon during the week?

_____

_____

When you read your Bible last, what did you read?

_____

_____

How have you applied those truths to your life?

_____

_____

_____

Now step back and look at your answers. How have you done on acting upon what you've heard? Which building are you establishing? The one built on a foundation of rock? Or the one built on sand?

 ## _Living Insights_

Go over each part of the Sermon on the Mount and see how much you are *doing* about what you've learned. In the space provided, check whether your life is resting solidly on each truth or whether it is resting on a foundation of sand.

Sermon of the Lord	Foundation of Your Life		Sermon of the Lord	Foundation of Your Life	
Truth	*Rock*	*Sand*	*Truth*	*Rock*	*Sand*
Chapter 5			Chapter 6		
v. 3	☐	☐	v. 1	☐	☐
v. 4	☐	☐	vv. 2–4	☐	☐
v. 5	☐	☐	vv. 5–15	☐	☐
v. 6	☐	☐	vv. 16–18	☐	☐
v. 7	☐	☐	vv. 19–24	☐	☐
v. 8	☐	☐	vv. 25–34	☐	☐
v. 9	☐	☐			
vv. 10–12	☐	☐			
vv. 13–16	☐	☐	Chapter 7		
v. 19	☐	☐	vv. 1–5	☐	☐
v. 20	☐	☐	v. 6	☐	☐
vv. 21–26	☐	☐	vv. 7–11	☐	☐
vv. 27–30	☐	☐	v. 12	☐	☐
vv. 31–32	☐	☐	vv. 13–14	☐	☐
vv. 33–37	☐	☐	vv. 15–23	☐	☐
vv. 38–42	☐	☐	vv. 24–27	☐	☐
vv. 43–48	☐	☐			

Step back and take another look at the life you're building. How solid is it? How safe is it from the storms of life? Where are you most vulnerable to a washout? What could you do to shore up that foundation? Take some time now to go before your Father with these questions and concerns, for He is the Master Builder and holds the blueprints for your life.

BOOKS FOR
PROBING FURTHER

If you came away discouraged from the Living Insights in our last lesson, condemning the property and demolishing the building is not the answer. Moving the building onto a more solid foundation, though, is. If the foundation of your life is on shaky ground, you might want to check out a few of these building manuals to see what you need to do to solve that problem. They are excellent books. Hear what they have to say. But remember, hearing *alone* won't get the job done. You're going to have to roll up your sleeves and *do* something about what you hear.

Commentaries

Barclay, William. *The Gospel of Matthew,* vol. 1. Revised edition. The Daily Study Bible series. Philadelphia, Pa.: Westminster Press, 1975. This commentary covers the first ten chapters of Matthew with half of the text dealing with the Sermon on the Mount. Barclay's unique contribution as a commentator stems from the breadth of historical background from which he draws. Very readable and nontechnical.

Carson, D. A. "Matthew." In *The Expositor's Bible Commentary,* vol. 8. Edited by Frank E. Gaebelein. Grand Rapids, Mich.: Zondervan Publishing House, Regency Reference Library, 1984. This commentary draws from a wide variety of sources to illuminate Matthew's text, including theological studies, linguistic studies, and both ancient and current commentaries. It is a balanced blend of scholarly research aimed primarily at equipping the biblical expositor.

Hendriksen, William. *Exposition of the Gospel According to Matthew.* New Testament Commentary series. Grand Rapids, Mich.: Baker Book House, 1973. Less technical than *The Expositor's Bible Commentary,* this work is helpful for the layperson as well as the more serious student of the Bible. The Greek and Hebrew words are referred to judiciously, and his cross-referencing to other biblical texts is extensive and extremely helpful.

Stott, John R. W. *The Message of the Sermon on the Mount (Matthew 5–7)*. Revised edition of *Christian Counter-Culture*. The Bible Speaks Today series. Downers Grove, Ill.: InterVarsity Press, 1978. This excellent work is without peer in its treatment of the Sermon on the Mount. Stott is a respected evangelical scholar of international renown and has given us the best single volume available on this subject. The scholarship is broad and deep, yet the author has managed to make the writing not only accessible to a large audience but compelling as well.

Theological Studies

Luther, Martin. *The Sermon on the Mount Sermons* and *The Magnificat*, vol. 21. Edited by Jaroslav Pelikan. *Luther's Works*. St. Louis, Mo.: Concordia Publishing House, 1956. Through the centuries, this work by the famous German reformer has remained a popular classic. A very readable commentary, it sparkles with wit and relevance and is supported by strong pillars of logic, theology, and insightful illustrations.

General Expositions

Lloyd-Jones, D. Martyn. *Studies in the Sermon on the Mount*. Grand Rapids, Mich.: William B. Eerdmans Publishing Co., 1971. Although wordy and, in places, rambling, this work still stands as a valuable addition in the library of anyone wanting to study the Sermon on the Mount. The author's eye is always on Scripture and life, balancing his exposition of the text with practical applications.

Sermon Collections

Lucado, Max. *The Applause of Heaven*. Dallas, Tex.: Word Publishing, 1990. A compilation of the pastor's sermons on the Beatitudes, this work is beautifully written and offers a fragrant potpourri of stories, illustrations, and modern applications.

Thielicke, Helmut. *Life Can Begin Again*. Translated by John W. Doberstein. London, England: James Clarke and Co., 1963. Written a generation ago by the famed German theologian, this book is neither commentary nor exposition nor theology. Rather, it is a book of the author's sermons on the Sermon on the Mount. It is full of insights and practical application.

Topical Studies

Character

Crabb, Larry. *Inside Out*. Colorado Springs, Colo.: NavPress, 1988. Based on Christ's scathing criticism of the Pharisees in Matthew 23:25–28, this book examines, from a psychologist's perspective, what it takes to develop Christlike character from the inside out.

Materialism

White, John. *The Golden Cow: Materialism in the Twentieth-Century Church*. Downers Grove, Ill.: InterVarsity Press, 1979. Much of what Jesus says in His sermon deals in some way with the human heart's struggle with materialism. The author first deals with this issue on an individual level, then on an institutional church level. His study is both convincing and convicting, much like Jesus' own words.

Prayer

Bounds, E. M. *The Complete Works of E. M. Bounds on Prayer*. Grand Rapids, Mich.: Baker Book House, 1990. A collection of eight books, this work is a gold mine of the author's thoughts and feelings about prayer. His books are recognized by many as classics on the subject and form a stimulating companion to Jesus' words on prayer in Matthew 6:5–15.

Sexual Sin

White, John. *Eros Defiled: The Christian and Sexual Sin*. Downers Grove, Ill.: InterVarsity Press, 1977. Adultery and the lust that fans its flames are two of the many sensitive topics Jesus dealt with in the Sermon on the Mount. Psychologist John White deals with these issues and other forms of sexual sin in this work, which is uncompromising in its biblical convictions yet unparalleled in its compassion. A book that truly reflects the character of Christ, "full of grace and truth" (John 1:14).

Some of the books listed here may be out of print and available only through a library. All of these works are recommended reading only. With the exception of books by Charles R. Swindoll, none of them are available through Insight for Living. If you wish to obtain some of these suggested readings, please contact your local Christian bookstore.

ORDERING INFORMATION

Cassette Tapes and Study Guide

This Bible study guide was designed to be used independently or in conjunction with the broadcast of Chuck Swindoll's taped messages on the topic listed below. If you would like to order cassette tapes or further copies of this study guide, please see the information given below and the Order Form provided on the last page of this guide.

SIMPLE FAITH

Real Christianity. Where is it? What does it look like? Surprisingly, a great many Christians are wondering that these days. Especially those who once based their faith on the solid foundation of Jesus Christ but have since become trapped in the rat race of performance-based faith . . . caged by the self-imposed demands of works and more works. As a result, many now wonder, "What *is* real Christianity?"

Simple Faith isn't about adding more religious demands to an already complicated existence. It's about gaining freedom from tyrannical expectations and rediscovering the beauty of what Christ really taught. It's about getting out of the cage and winging your way back to freedom, peace, and rest in Jesus Christ—back to the life of simple faith He taught and, more importantly, He lived. It's the real message of the Sermon on the Mount, what it means to live an authentic, uncomplicated life. In short, it is a call to simple faith.

			Calif.*	U.S.	B.C.*	Canada*
SPF	SG	Study Guide	$ 5.31	$ 4.95	$ 6.37	$ 6.37
SPF	CS	Cassette series, includes album cover	42.56	39.50	60.31	57.29
SPF	1–7	Individual cassettes, include messages A and B	5.36	5.00	7.61	7.23

*These prices already include the following charges: for delivery in **California,** applicable sales tax; **Canada,** 7% GST and 7% postage and handling (on tapes only); **British Columbia,** 7% GST, 6% British Columbia sales tax (on tapes only), and 7% postage and handling (on tapes only). The prices are subject to change without notice.

SPF   1-A: *Let's Keep it Simple*—Survey of Matthew 5–7
         B: *The Qualities of Simple Faith*—Matthew 5:1–12

SPF   2-A: *A Simple Counterstrategy: Shake and Shine*—
            Matthew 5:13–16
         B: *Simplicity Starts from Within*—Matthew 5:17–26; 15:1–20

SPF   3-A: *Simple Instructions on Serious Issues*—Matthew 5:27–37;
            19:3, 7–8
         B: *Simple Advice to the Selfish and Strong-willed*—
            Matthew 5:38–48

SPF   4-A: *Beware! Religious Performance Now Showing*—
            Matthew 6:1–8; Micah 6:6–8
         B: *Prayer and Fasting Minus All the Pizzazz*—Matthew 6:9–18

SPF   5-A: *When Simple Faith Erodes*—Matthew 6:19–24
         B: *The Subtle Enemy of Simple Faith*—Matthew 6:25–34;
            Luke 10:38–42

SPF   6-A: *If You're Serious about Simple Faith, Stop This!*—
            Matthew 7:1–5; Galatians 6:1
         B: *The Most Powerful of All Four-letter Words*—
            Matthew 7:6–12

SPF   7-A: *Simple Yet Serious Warnings for Complicated Times*—
            Matthew 7:13–23
          B: *The Simple Secret of an Unsinkable Life*—Matthew 7:24–29

How to Order by Mail

Simply mark on the order form whether you want the series or individual tapes. Mail the form with your payment to the appropriate address listed below. We will process your order as promptly as we can.

United States: Mail your order to the Sales Department at Insight for Living, Post Office Box 69000, Anaheim, California 92817-0900. If you wish your order to be shipped first-class for faster delivery, add 10 percent of the total order amount. Otherwise, please allow four to six weeks for delivery by fourth-class mail. We accept personal checks, money orders, Visa, or MasterCard in payment for materials. Unfortunately, we are unable to offer invoicing or COD orders.

Canada: Mail your order to Insight for Living Ministries, Post Office Box 2510, Vancouver, British Columbia V6B 3W7. Allow approximately four weeks for delivery. We accept personal checks, money orders, Visa, or MasterCard in payment for materials. Unfortunately, we are unable to offer invoicing or COD orders.

Australia, New Zealand, or Papua New Guinea: Mail your order to Insight for Living, Inc., GPO Box 2823 EE, Melbourne, Victoria 3001, Australia. Please allow six to ten weeks for delivery by surface mail. If you would like your order sent airmail, the delivery time may be reduced. Using the United States price as a base, add postage costs—surface or airmail—to the amount of your order. Please use the chart that follows to determine correct postage. Due to fluctuating currency rates, we can accept only personal checks made payable in U.S. funds, international money orders, Visa, or MasterCard in payment for materials.

Overseas: Other overseas residents should mail their orders to our United States office. Please allow six to ten weeks for delivery by surface mail. If you would like your order sent airmail, the delivery time may be reduced. Using the United States price as a base, add postage costs—surface or airmail—to the amount of your order. Please use the chart that follows to determine correct postage. Due to fluctuating currency rates, we can accept only personal checks made payable in U.S. funds, international money orders, Visa, or MasterCard in payment for materials.

Type of Postage	Postage Cost
Surface	10% of total order
Airmail	25% of total order

For Faster Service, Order by Telephone or FAX

For Visa or MasterCard orders, you are welcome to use one of our toll-free numbers between the hours of 7:00 A.M. and 4:30 P.M., Pacific time, Monday through Friday, or our FAX numbers. The numbers to use from anywhere in the United States are **1-800-772-8888** or FAX (714) 575-5049. To order from Canada, call our Vancouver office using **1-800-663-7639** or FAX (604) 596-2975. Vancouver residents, call (604) 596-2910. Australian residents should phone (03) 872-4606. From overseas, call our Sales Department at (714) 575-5000 in the United States.

Our Guarantee

Our cassettes are guaranteed for ninety days against faulty performance or breakage due to a defect in the tape. For best results, please be sure your tape recorder is in good operating condition and is cleaned regularly.

Note: To cover processing and handling, there is a $10 fee for *any* returned check.

Order Form

SPF CS represents the entire *Simple Faith* series in a special album cover, while SPF 1–7 are the individual tapes included in the series. SPF SG represents this study guide, should you desire to order additional copies.

Item	Calif.*	Unit Price U.S.	B.C.*	Canada*	Quantity	Amount
SPF CS	$42.56	$39.50	$60.31	$57.29		$
SPF 1	5.36	5.00	7.61	7.23		
SPF 2	5.36	5.00	7.61	7.23		
SPF 3	5.36	5.00	7.61	7.23		
SPF 4	5.36	5.00	7.61	7.23		
SPF 5	5.36	5.00	7.61	7.23		
SPF 6	5.36	5.00	7.61	7.23		
SPF 7	5.36	5.00	7.61	7.23		
SPF SG	5.31	4.95	6.37	6.37		
					Subtotal	
			Overseas Residents Pay U.S. price plus 10% surface postage or 25% airmail. Also, see "How to Order by Mail."			
			U.S. First-Class Shipping For faster delivery, add 10% for postage and handling.			
			Gift to Insight for Living Tax-deductible in the United States and Canada.			
			Total Amount Due Please do not send cash.			$

If there is a balance: ☐ apply it as a donation ☐ please refund
*These prices already include applicable taxes and shipping costs.

Payment by: ☐ Check or money order made payable to Insight for Living or

☐ Credit card (circle one): Visa   MasterCard   Number _____

   Expiration Date _____   Signature _____
   We cannot process your credit card purchase without your signature.

Name _____

Address _____

City _____ State/Province _____

Zip/Postal Code _____   Country _____

Telephone ( ) _____ Radio Station ___ ___ ___ ___
   If questions arise concerning your order, we may need to contact you.

Mail this order form to the Sales Department at one of these addresses:
Insight for Living, Post Office Box 69000, Anaheim, CA 92817-0900
Insight for Living Ministries, Post Office Box 2510, Vancouver, BC, Canada V6B 3W7
Insight for Living, Inc., GPO Box 2823 EE, Melbourne, VIC 3001, Australia